Operations and Technology Express

George Green

OPERATIONS

06.01

- Fast track route to mastering the management of operations and technology

- Covers the key areas of operations and technology, from operating systems and managing resources to quality and environmental awareness

- Examples and lessons from some of the world's most successful businesses, including Egg, Nissan, easyJet, Ford, British Airways and Nestle, and ideas from the smartest thinkers, including W Edwards Deming, Joseph Juran, Kaoru Ishikawa, Philip Crosby, Tom Peters and Charles Handy

- Includes a glossary of key concepts and a comprehensive resources guide

>>EXPRESS EXEC.COM<<
essential management thinking at your fingertips

The right of George Green to be identified as the author of this work has been asserted in accordance with the Copyright, Designs and Patents Act 1988

First published 2002 by
Capstone Publishing (A Wiley Company)
8 Newtec Place
Magdalen Road
Oxford OX4 1RE
United Kingdom
http://www.capstoneideas.com

CIP catalogue records for this book are available from the British Library and the US Library of Congress

ISBN 1-84112-249-1

This book is printed on acid-free paper

Substantial discounts on bulk quantities of Capstone books are available to corporations, professional associations and other organizations. Please contact Capstone for more details on +44 (0)1865 798 623 or (fax) +44 (0)1865 240 941 or (e-mail) info@wiley-capstone.co.uk

Contents

Introduction to ExpressExec

ExpressExec is 3 million words of the latest management thinking compiled into 10 modules. Each module contains 10 individual titles forming a comprehensive resource of current business practice written by leading practitioners in their field. From brand management to balanced scorecard, ExpressExec enables you to grasp the key concepts behind each subject and implement the theory immediately. Each of the 100 titles is available in print and electronic formats.

Through the ExpressExec.com Website you will discover that you can access the complete resource in a number of ways:

» printed books or e-books;
» e-content – PDF or XML (for licensed syndication) adding value to an intranet or Internet site;
» a corporate e-learning/knowledge management solution providing a cost-effective platform for developing skills and sharing knowledge within an organization;
» bespoke delivery – tailored solutions to solve your need.

Why not visit www.expressexec.com and register for free key management briefings, a monthly newsletter and interactive skills checklists. Share your ideas about ExpressExec and your thoughts about business today.

Please contact elound@wiley-capstone.co.uk for more information.

Introduction to Operations and Technology

Considers the role of operations and technology in the modern world of business. It stresses:

» the growing importance of managing operations and introducing technology as organizations strive for success in an ever more competitive environment; and

» the concepts apply to any type of organization, whether seeking profits or not.

"If it ain't broke, you just haven't looked hard enough. Fix it anyway."

So wrote Tom Peters, in *Thriving on Chaos* (1987). And really, that sums up operations and technology nicely. It's all about continually seeking to do things in new, more effective ways, with the help of new technology, as it becomes available.

The use of operational processes and the application of new technology is not a new phenomenon. After all, the pyramids were conceived, planned and built in Egypt many thousands of years ago with the latest technology available, as was the Parthenon in Athens. And both were built to last!

We can also see, through the ages, how the introduction of some new technological discoveries had a profound effect not only on industry but also on the way people lived their lives. Examples include the introduction of the wheel, the printing press, the telegraph, the telephone, the steam engine, the internal combustion engine, the postal service, the radio and television, radar, the jet engine, satellite communications systems, the computer and, of course, the Internet.

The most recent advance concerns the linking of the computer with the television, the satellite and the telephone, which promises to reshape a number of the operational processes that we have used so successfully during the latter part of the twentieth century and the beginning of the twenty-first century. The introduction of e-mail and e-commerce is having a profound effect on operational processes throughout a wide range of industries and also upon the way people interact with each other, both in their personal and business relationships.

In this book we will be looking at some of the operational concepts that have been identified and developed over the last century up to the current day and the contribution they have made to our understanding of the operations process. We will be examining how the concepts have made a difference to the way we produce both manufactured and service products and why they will continue to make a difference in the future.

The combined effect of the technological advances over the last century has been to make world markets more accessible than they have ever been before. This results in more organizations operating in the global market place, which increases competition between them. In order to gain competitive advantage, they need to focus more and more upon how they can use their resources more effectively to improve the quality of their products and to reduce their costs.

Just as the global market place brings more competition, however, it also provides more choice about how and where organizations carry out their operations. This will be explored further in Chapter 5.

This need to focus on the effective use of resources also applies to not-for-profit organizations such as charities, many of which find themselves having to compete for financial support against a much wider range of "competitors" than ever before. The introduction of the National Lottery in the UK, for example, had a significant effect on the revenues of many other charity organizations as people played the new lottery with the pound coin they would previously have dropped into the collector's box.

The World Wide Fund for Nature reacted to this increased competition in the early 1990s by introducing a facility for donors to target their monetary gifts at specific projects that they wanted to support, such as a particular species of animal.

In many cases, schools now have to compete for pupils on the basis of the quality and value for money of the teaching they provide. There are even league tables of the schools that have performed best, though there is generally some controversy over which criteria should be included in the calculations.

The result is that all organizations have to keep on looking for better ways of using the resources that are available to them. In these fiercely competitive times, it's not just about gaining a competitive edge; it's also about survival.

Definition of Terms: What is Operations?

Sets out the classic definitions of operations. It considers:

» operations as a system of inputs and outputs;
» the various types of inputs;
» the transformation process;
» design and conformance quality; and
» the relationship between operations and marketing.

There are two main strands to operations. First, it is the process of delivering promises to customers. These promises may be made by any type of organization:

» a commercial company delivering its advertised manufactured products;
» a commercial company delivering its advertised service products;
» a university turning out well educated graduates; and
» a charitable organization supporting good causes.

Peter Drucker (1991)[1] suggests that performance and results are very important in not-for-profit organizations and that they are probably more difficult to control than in commercially driven ones.

The *key concepts* in delivering the promises tend to be around quality, availability and deadlines. The *main risks* center on:

» the product not being of acceptable quality, leading either to rejection by the customer or to failure during its use; and
» the product being unavailable at the outlets promised, meaning that the customer is unable to buy it or to use it.

The second major dimension to the term operations relates to the control of the amount of resources that are used to deliver the promise. This means that all of the resources need to be available in the right places, in the right quantities, at the right time and at the right cost. The *key concepts* here tend to be concerned with planning and forecasting, capacity management, operating systems, information management and supply management. The *main risks* center on:

» too many resources being used, resulting in higher costs and lower profitability;
» different parts of the operation running at different capacity levels, leading to bottlenecks and inefficient operations;
» inappropriate operating systems being used which do not allow the product to be produced in the required quantities;
» information not being passed on to the appropriate people, leading to errors or delays; and
» inadequate control of supplies, leading to materials/resource shortages.

Operations (often called production) is a term that can be used at several levels.

» Most large organizations have a specific department, known as the operations or production department, under the control of the operations (or production) manager, which focuses on delivering the products of the organization. This will be a core part of the business, which will work to the specifications laid down by the marketing department. It will have responsibility for all aspects relating to production of the products.

» Some organizations, especially smaller ones, may not have a specialized operations department but they will still be organized and structured in such a way that someone has responsibility for delivering the core product.

» Every department within an organization has a core product of its own (for example, the finance department manages budgets and controls payments on behalf of other departments). Each department, therefore, needs to ensure that its own operational processes are in place to ensure that their products are delivered to their own internal customers with the appropriate quality standards being met and with the resources employed efficiently.

» Each person, whatever job they are doing, produces an end product (or, more usually, a range of end products) either for someone within their organization (their internal customer) or for someone outside the organization (their external customer). Whatever anyone does for any of their customers can be termed their product and the operational concepts can be applied to the activities that the person carries out. For example, an administrator in the human resources department may be asked to supply information about staffing levels to someone in the finance department. The same concepts relating to quality standards, economic use of resources and delivery deadlines could also be applied to this specific transaction.

At its most basic, the operations process can be regarded as a system with the elements as shown in Figure 2.1.

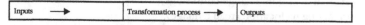

Inputs ⟶	Transformation process ⟶	Outputs

Fig. 2.1 The operations process.

INPUTS

Inputs include *the resources that will be processed*, which will usually consist of:

» materials (either raw or semi-finished);
» information (raw data or information); and
» the customer.

Inputs also include *the resources that will be used to process them*, such as:

» plant and machinery;
» buildings;
» computers;
» planned systems and processes;
» people (and their skills) who operate the plant/machinery/computers and apply the systems and processes;
» people who provide administrative backup (for example training);
» suppliers;
» vehicles;
» finance; and
» ideas and innovation.

THE TRANSFORMATION PROCESS

The transformation process relates to the way in which the inputs are changed. Slack *et al* (2001)[2] identify the following types of transformation process.

Materials processing

Materials processing might involve:

» transforming an item's physical properties (for example, raw materials such as gold changed into rings);
» changing its location (road haulage);
» transferring its ownership (retail outlets); and
» storing it (safety deposit boxes).

Information processing

Information processing could involve:

» transforming raw data into useful information (such as carrying out a survey and producing a meaningful report);
» changing the location of the information (the Internet);
» changing possession of the information (offering a report for sale or passing it on to another department which may need it); and
» storing the information (a records depository or a library).

Customer processing

Customer processing may involve:

» changing the way the customer looks (for example, a tailor will make them look more stylish and well dressed);
» transferring them to a different location (a train or a taxi);
» accommodating the customer (a hotel);
» improving their physiological state (a health club); or
» enhancing their psychological state (various types of entertainment or restaurants).

OUTPUTS

Outputs include both desired outputs such as finished products, and less desirable outputs such as faulty products, rejects and waste.

It should be noted that, in many cases, the end product of the process, whether it is a desired or a less desirable output, will become an input to another operations process. For example, a manufacturer of car seats will pass on their finished product, the seat, to the vehicle assembler where it will become an input into the final production of a complete car.

Similarly, faulty products and rejects will go back into the process to be reworked and will become inputs once again.

Even waste materials will form an input for the waste disposal operator, though, as we will see in Chapter 7, many organizations go to great lengths to ensure that waste is kept to a minimum or recycled. The quality of the inputs used will clearly affect the quality of the outputs produced during the transformation process. We will be looking at quality in more detail in Chapter 6, but at this point it is useful to recognize the two main types of quality:

» design quality; and
» conformance quality.

Design quality

Design quality relates to the features in the product that give it a high quality feel, which make it attractive to customers who are seeking extra comfort, extra facilities or greater exclusivity.

Thus deluxe hotels like Raffles in Singapore, or the Peninsular in Hong Kong, offer more facilities than a two star hotel. A first class train seat on Eurostar between Paris and London offers more comfort than a second class seat. These additional features are designed into the product in response to identified customer needs or wants.

Conformance quality

Conformance quality, on the other hand, relates to whether the product does what it promised to do. Thus, a second class train seat, which allows the customer to reach their destination safely and with a reasonable amount of comfort, has reached the same level of conformance quality as the first class seat.

Similarly, the two star hotel, which offers a more basic service, but provides all of the services that it promised will reach the same level of conformance quality as the deluxe hotel.

In both cases, the product did what it was designed to do and could, therefore, be considered as fit for the purpose. Clearly, both types of quality are important when considering the operations process.

A product with a very high level of design quality, such as a meal at a Michelin starred restaurant, will require inputs of a high design quality. This means choosing the freshest vegetables and highest quality meat and fish. It will also mean employing the most skilled chefs to transform the ingredients into the finished meal and the most skilled serving staff to deliver it to the customer. It will also be necessary to use a process during the transformation stage that will allow the chef to give individual attention to each meal to ensure that conformance quality is maintained.

At a fast food restaurant, on the other hand, which offers a lower design quality, the customer is not expecting such a gastronomic delight and the design quality of the ingredients may not have to be so high, or the staff so skilled. The process used during the transformation stage may be more focused on achieving a volume of throughput of good quality meals delivered to the customer in a very short waiting time. The food, will, however, still need to be tasty and what the customer expected.

We mentioned above that the role of operations is to deliver the promises made by the organization, while at the same time ensuring that resources are used in the most effective way to keep costs down. These promises are usually made by the marketing function, or whoever has responsibility for identifying customer requirements. This often leads to ongoing tension between the marketing and operations functions as shown in Figure 2.2.

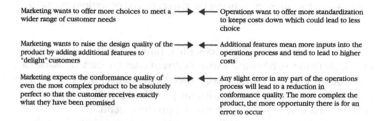

Marketing wants to offer more choices to meet a wider range of customer needs ⟶ ⟵ Operations want to offer more standardization to keeps costs down which could lead to less choice

Marketing wants to raise the design quality of the product by adding additional features to "delight" customers ⟶ ⟵ Additional features mean more inputs into the operations process and tend to lead to higher costs

Marketing expects the conformance quality of even the most complex product to be absolutely perfect so that the customer receives exactly what they have been promised ⟶ ⟵ Any slight error in any part of the operations process will lead to a reduction in conformance quality. The more complex the product, the more opportunity there is for an error to occur

Fig. 2.2 Tension between the marketing and operations functions.

For example, offering three engine sizes of a particular model of car means that materials supply lines have to be set up for each one and the manufacturing process may have to be set up differently for each size. Similarly, offering additional features such as CD players, extra safety air bags and rear spoilers leads to additional inputs being introduced into the process and, therefore to increased costs. In addition, both situations may lead to a more complex and prolonged operations process and increase the possibility of error, leading to a loss of conformance quality.

Although it is suggested above that an increase in quality will tend to increase pressure on costs, many successful organizations have managed to offer high quality products at low prices because they have used processes that keep rejects, faults and waste to a minimum, thus reducing their operating costs. We will discover later in Chapter 6 that the issue is not one of choosing either low cost *or* good quality, rather one of achieving both low cost *and* good quality.

Let's consider two further tensions between the marketing and operations functions in Figure 2.3.

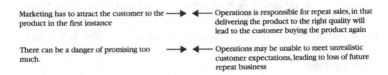

Marketing has to attract the customer to the product in the first instance ⟶ ⟵ Operations is responsible for repeat sales, in that delivering the product to the right quality will lead to the customer buying the product again

There can be a danger of promising too much. ⟶ ⟵ Operations may be unable to meet unrealistic customer expectations, leading to loss of future repeat business

Fig. 2.3 Further tensions between the marketing and operations functions.

Research has shown that it costs five times as much to gain a new customer than to do business with a current one. So, clearly, marketing and operations must work closely together because, if the operations process is not capable of delivering the promised product, the customer will be dissatisfied and will not use the product again.

The UK based Virgin Airlines identifies every month the top ten issues that are most commented on by their customers, either as criticism or praise. These are identified from telephone and face-to-face conversations, feedback forms and customer complaints. All of these issues are discussed at senior level each month and act as driving forces for change in the way the airline carries out its operations.

In order to complete the transformation process, most organizations will use technology to help them.

TECHNOLOGY

We can define technology as being the tools, machines and implements that we use during the operations process. It may be a very simple tool such as a pen and a diary with which you record your future activities, or a relatively complex one such as a computerized diary system networked with those of your colleagues, in which you all store your activities.

Technology can be used in any part of the operations process, such as:

» storing school examination results;
» loading raw materials into a hopper ready for processing;
» carrying out a service, such as digging a garden with a spade;
» molding or cutting materials on a machine in a factory; and
» delivering the finished product, whether electronically such as in the telecommunications industry, or physically as in the transport industry.

New technology can be found in any type of organization. In fact, some not-for-profit organizations such as hospitals often have very complex equipment of the very latest designs.

In the early 1990s, the Far East based Taj Group introduced a very powerful database system on which it could maintain and update information on customer preferences in their various hotels; this could relate to their choice of room or menu, or their requirements for communication facilities. This allowed the hotels in the group to be ready to provide excellent customer service for its customers.

KEY LEARNING POINTS

» Operational concepts apply to all types of operation.
» They apply at several levels.
» The operations process consists of inputs, transformation and outputs.
» There are two main types of quality: design and conformance.
» Technology can be used in any part of the operations process.

NOTES

1 Drucker, P. *et al.* (1991) *Managing the Non-Profit Organization: Principles and Practices, Harper Business*, New York.
2 Slack, N. *et al.* (2001) Operations Management, Pitman, Harlow.

The Evolution of Operations

The modern day concepts of operations have grown out of the thinking of a number of people over the last century. This chapter examines how the concepts have evolved. It includes:

» the early days of scientific management;
» the moves towards a more people orientated approach;
» the focus on quality;
» attitudes towards stock/inventory;
» the focus on the customer;
» the impact of technology; and
» the flexible approach to operations in the modern era.

In this section we can look at how concepts in operations have developed over the years. These developments have largely been driven by four main factors:

» the need to compete with other organizations as ease of travel, transport and communications allowed more companies access to larger markets;
» new developments in technology, such as the introduction of the microprocessor, e-mail and the Internet;
» the need to increase profits for shareholders in the face of fierce competition, thus putting pressure on cost reduction; and
» the recognition of the part that motivated staff can play in achieving results for the organization.

We can identify the following developments in operational concepts, all of which have influenced the way in which organizations operate today:

» the industrial revolution (late seventeenth – late nineteenth century);
» scientific management (1898);
» organization and structure (1900);
» human relations management (1924);
» focus on quality (1950s);
» operations as a system (1970s);
» questions about inventory (1970s);
» focus on the customer (1970s);
» wide application of the microprocessor (1980s);
» the flexible organization (1990s); and
» the advance of e-technology and the Internet (1990s).

Let's briefly consider each in turn.

THE INDUSTRIAL REVOLUTION

Before the introduction of machinery during the industrial revolution, most goods and services were produced by the skills of an individual person or group of people. The introduction of new machines replaced the need for these skills by building them into their systems. In many cases they also reduced the need for people to be employed, as one or two machine operators could produce many times the work that individuals had previously been able to do.

SCIENTIFIC MANAGEMENT

The first major step in the introduction of some of the operations management processes that we still recognize today was the focus on time and method study by Frederick W. Taylor (1856-1915), which was known as scientific management.

Although scientific management has largely been replaced through-out the developed countries by a greater focus on motivation of the workforce, time and method study can still be seen in many modern day operations. Many services are still quoted for in "time rate" terms; for example, standard automobile services are all timed at so many hours' work. You can learn more about F.W. Taylor in Chapter 8.

Frank G. Gilbreth (1868-1924) also focused on scientific manage-ment and together with his wife, Lillie M. Gilbreth (1878-1972), worked towards finding "the one best way" of carrying out specific tasks. He is said to have remarked: "the greatest waste in the world comes from needless, ill directed and ineffective motions."

Henry L. Gantt (1861-1919) was a contemporary of the Gilbreths and Taylor; he designed the Gantt chart in 1917 for planning and measuring progress towards the completion of planned activities. This type of chart is still very popular today and there are a number of software applications that apply Gantt charts to control projects.

ORGANIZATION AND STRUCTURE

Two European writers focused on managing the people and the work in an organization rather than analyzing individual tasks as Taylor and the Gilbreths had done. They looked at how organizations should be set up and structured. Henri Fayol (1841-1925) set out the main activities of any organization and in 1916 was the first to identify "management" as a specific activity. The six activities were:

» technical (including production);
» commercial;

» financial (procuring capital);
» security;
» accounting (profit and loss, balance sheet etc.); and
» managerial.

He broke down the managerial activity into five further functions:

» planning;
» organizing;
» commanding;
» coordinating; and
» controlling.

Fayol went on to identify 14 principles of management, some of which have particular relevance to the study of operations:

» there should be division of labor to allow specialization;
» remuneration for work should be fair;
» individuals should be allowed to use their initiative;
» operations with the same objective should have one manager and one plan; and
» there should be a clear line of authority.

Max Weber (1864-1920) identified the characteristics of the ideal "bureaucracy,"[1] a word he used as a label for the most effective management system. He, too, stresses:

» division of labor; and
» clear line of authority.

As a result of the work of these two writers we can see the origins of the operations department.

HUMAN RELATIONS MANAGEMENT

Elton Mayo (1880-1949) looked at the human aspect of work, considering how people reacted to their working conditions and how important job satisfaction was. He carried out a series of experiments over a period of eight years from 1924-32 at the former Hawthorne

Works of the Western Electric Company (which eventually became AT&T).

The experiments clearly showed that money was not the only important factor in improving productivity, because he found that workers are motivated by many other things, such as:

» the amount of responsibility people have;
» how much they can organize their own work; and
» the amount of social interaction that takes place.

You can learn more about these experiments in Chapter 8.

Abraham Maslow (1943)[2] and Frederick Herzberg (1964)[3] and many other major writers also focus on motivating the workforce. Maslow identified a hierarchy of human needs:

» physiological;
» security;
» social;
» esteem; and
» self actualization.

He suggested that once a lower need was satisfied, the individual would be motivated by the next higher need in the hierarchy.

Herzberg set out a two-factor theory, suggesting that there were factors that motivated people (motivators) and other factors (hygienes), which would not particularly motivate, but would lead to dissatisfaction if they were not adequately provided. Among the former he included:

» how interesting the work itself is;
» achievement;
» recognition;
» responsibility; and
» advancement.

Among the latter he identified:

» company policy;
» the way people are supervised;
» salary;
» interpersonal relations; and
» the working conditions.

Most successful companies now recognize the value of the human relations approach.

FOCUS ON QUALITY

From the middle of the last century, a number of very distinguished consultants and writers focused their thoughts upon how to improve quality. The adoption of their various ideas eventually resulted in the concept of Total Quality Management (TQM).

Dr W. Edwards Deming, though an American, was largely instrumental in the revival and success of Japanese industry during the 1950s. He later set out a 14-point plan for quality improvement, which is summarized in Chapter 8.

Philip Crosby pioneered the idea of "getting things right first time" and "zero defects." He introduced the concept that "quality is free" by showing how the avoidance of having to put right what has gone wrong can result in high quality products at low cost. In the latter part of the twentieth century the Japanese, particularly in their manufacturing industries, created an export boom by using this approach to produce high quality goods at low prices.

Joseph M. Juran stressed that the definition of quality in any product should be not only that it conforms to specification but also that it should be "fit for use," which meant that any product which had harmful effects could not meet the definition.

Kaoru Ishikawa focused on the usefulness of quality circles, which were used extensively in Japan. He also introduced the "cause and effect diagram" as a systematic technique for diagnosing and analyzing quality problems. You can see an example of this in Chapter 8.

OPERATIONS AS A SYSTEM

During the last quarter of the twentieth century the classic model of the operations process of inputs, transformation and outputs (which we saw in Chapter 2) began to emerge. In 1985 Wild identified four types of transformation process:

» physical change;
» change in ownership;

» change in location; and
» change in the state of the customer.

This was built upon by Slack *et al* (2001) into the model we saw in Chapter 2.

QUESTIONS ABOUT INVENTORY

In the 1970s, people began to focus on the management of materials. Until this time, manufacturing organizations in particular, had stored large quantities of materials in preparation for use in their operations processes. It was gradually realized that an enormous amount of capital was required to fund the purchase of the materials, which might lie unused for some time, and the secure storage of the materials against theft, deterioration and obsolescence.

This led to the introduction of sophisticated materials management systems such as just-in-time, and the materials requirements planning systems MRP I and MRP II, all of which we shall look at in more detail in Chapter 6.

At the same time, improvements in delivery and logistics services, which began to offer next day, and even same day delivery, meant that organizations no longer needed to keep vital (and expensive) spares to ensure that their plant and machinery could be repaired quickly.

FOCUS ON THE CUSTOMER

Also during the 1970s, there came a realization that competitive advantage could be gained by listening more closely to what customers wanted and trying to satisfy their needs. Organizations began to be much more "customer driven" and focused their energies on creating more choice and changing the products to more closely match what the customer wanted.

Thus, autos were made in a whole range of different models; transport services began to offer timetables reflecting the times customers wanted to travel; tour operators began to offer a range of holidays to reflect customer preferences. As we saw in Chapter 2, this began to put additional pressure on the operations function, as any move away from standardization tends to increase complexity and may affect costs.

In 1982 Peters and Waterman analyzed the most successful companies in the US and produced a blueprint of eight attributes that they had in common. Four of these have particular relevance to the operations function:

» "closeness to the customer," which suggests that excellent companies get to know what their customers want and build up close relationships with them;
» "hands on, value driven," which suggests that managers should keep in touch with what is going on within the organization ("management by wandering about") to ensure that their customers are receiving the best value;
» "productivity through people," which very much supports the human relations theorists who saw motivating people as the key to delivering outstanding products; and
» "stick to the knitting," which suggests focusing on those things the organization does really well.

Kenichi Ohmae, in *The Mind of The Strategists* (1982),[4] suggests that a good strategy is one by which an organization can "gain significant ground on its competitors at an acceptable cost to itself." The organization needs to focus on three areas:

» its customers;
» its competitors; and
» its company.

So, organizations need to do things for their customers, better than their competitors can do them, ad within the capabilities of the organization. Ohmae advocates identifying the key success factors that are important to customers and delivering them effectively.

Tom Peters, in *Thriving on Chaos* (1987),[5] introduces the phrase "fail forward," which suggests that, in the current highly competitive environment, a new product should be "tested in situ" as he calls it, without waiting until exhaustive tests have been carried out. It should be tried out with real customers and, if any part of it doesn't work, then the organization should learn from its mistake and move forward armed with new knowledge. This would not, of course, be appropriate in any situation with a safety implication.

WIDE APPLICATION OF THE MICROPROCESSOR

During the late 1970s and early 1980s one of the major technological advances was the introduction of the microprocessor. This allowed manufactured products to be made smaller and with fewer moving parts. Items such as televisions could be made in large quantities at relatively low costs of production. Personal computers became possible.

We begin to find some parallels with the industrial revolution, which led at first to de-skilling of the workforce as jobs were replaced by machines. It became cheaper to replace some items that used to take great skill to repair when they went wrong.

In the same period robots were introduced into the operating process, though these tended to be very specialized and have not been introduced in anywhere near the quantities that people first imagined, and computer aided design and manufacture (CAD/CAM) also became embedded in operations processes.

THE FLEXIBLE ORGANIZATION

Charles Handy, in his book *The Age of Unreason* (1989)[6] explores, among other things, the shamrock organization, which may have more people working for it outside than within it. He describes the organization as a three-leafed shamrock made up of:

» core workers;
» outsourced services; and
» a flexible workforce.

Thus, a company might retain some core workers whose essential skills mean they are very much bound to the company's future success. It might, however, outsource some of its support services such as administration and training and could also hand some of its core production to a more flexible workforce, by buying in extra people when demand is high.

This shamrock approach allows the company to focus on its main products. It also puts the support activities into the hands of people expert at particular activities and allows the company itself to align production capacity with fluctuations in demand.

In the book Handy also introduces the concept of "upside down thinking," which suggests that we should turn some of our preconceived ideas on their heads. He asks, for example, why we shouldn't pay dentists in relation to the number of healthy mouths in their practice rather than on the repair work they do.

It is interesting that Handy refers to "unreason" and "upside down" while Tom Peters talks of "chaos." There is clearly something quite different about this era. One of the "chaotic" things that has happened is the blurring of the distinctions between customers, suppliers and competitors. Nowadays an organization may be supplied by a competitor or and customers may also be suppliers and suppliers customers. Different companies within larger organizations may even compete with each other.

Examples include British Airways carrying out engineering maintenance on Virgin Airlines airplanes, despite the intense rivalry between the companies on transatlantic routes. Another example can be taken from the UK National Health Service, which will, in certain circumstances, hire beds from private sector hospitals (its major competitor) if it needs to do so.

One further change is that instead of adopting a hierarchical structure organizations have moved to a team working approach in which people bring different types of expertise to a particular project. The teams may be fixed, or people may move between teams as they work on several projects at the same time. Team working allows an organization to respond more quickly and in these highly competitive times can often mean the difference between keeping and losing a customer.

ADVANCE OF E-TECHNOLOGY AND THE INTERNET

Like the industrial revolution, the e-revolution is having far reaching effects. Many organizations are seeking to move substantial parts of their business into an Internet operation.

The integration of telecommunications and the computer is still in its infancy at present and significant changes to the way we live our lives and the products we will use are at hand. The changes are happening very quickly. Only a few years ago, relatively few people had a personal computer; the same applies to the mobile phone. Now they exchange e-mails on mobile phones. This means that customers are now equipped with technology that is compatible with that used in company operations, so they can now be linked into the operations system and even become part of it.

The impact of the e-dimension will be the focus of the next chapter. Before moving on, we can set out some of the key advances in technology that were happening during the period mentioned above:

» spinning jenny 1764;
» steam engine 1769;
» first railroad 1830;
» phonograph 1877;
» automobile 1885;
» box camera 1885;
» radio 1895;
» first flight 1903;
» model T Ford 1908;
» first production line 1913;
» first non-stop transatlantic flight 1919;
» first regular television broadcasts 1939;
» computer 1946;
» first commercial jet flight 1952;
» Telstar satellite (linking US, Europe and Japan) 1962;
» mainframe computers developed 1960s–1980s;
» microprocessors developed 1970s–1980s;
» personal computers developed 1980s–1990s; and
» Internet 1990s.

KEY LEARNING POINTS

The following developments in operations theory have been identified:

» Industrial revolution.
» Scientific management.
» Organization and structure.
» Human relations management.
» Focus on quality.

> Operations as a system.
> Questions about inventory.
> Focus on the customer.
> Wide application of the microprocessor.
> The flexible organization.
> Advance of e-technology and the Internet.

NOTES

1 Weber, M. (1947) *The Theory of Social and Economic Organisation*, Oxford University Press, Oxford.
2 Maslow, A. (1943) "A theory of human motivation." *Psychological Review,* vol 50, No 4.
3 Herzberg, F. (1966) *Work and the Nature of Man*, Staples Press, New York.
4 Ohmae, K. (1982) *The Mind of The Strategists*, McGraw-Hill, New-York.
5 Peters, T. (1987) *Thriving on Chaos*, Pan Books, London.
6 Handy, C. (1989) *The Age of Unreason*, Business Books, London.

The E-Dimension

The Internet presents new challenges for operations. Chapter 4 explores the key issues, including:

» virtual operations;
» the advantages of on-line transactions;
» how some organizations use the Internet to gain competitive advantage; and
» case study: Egg.

In this chapter we will be looking at the impact of the Internet and its associated technology upon the operations function. There are several key advantages that it brings. It can:

» move the organization's shop window into the customer's living room so they can browse through their products in their own time and with little effort;
» reduce the requirements for premises;
» reduce the amount of stock needed to be held or allow its storage to be centralized;
» transfer some of the operational activities to the customer; and
» allow the customer to place an order without waiting in a queue.

Let's look at a number of industries and see what specific benefits it brings to them.

GENERAL RETAIL

Companies such as Amazon Books have built up huge businesses through selling on the Internet through their Websites. They don't have the costs of front line premises to incur, nor do they need to print brochures. The organization does still have to deliver the item, of course, though this can usually be done effectively either:

» from a central warehouse or warehouses, which reduces the need to keep stocks of the same item in a number of different places; or
» direct from the supplier, which means that the company never actually sees or handles the product and operating costs are reduced to an absolute minimum. The danger with this type of operation is that when a customer wants a repeat order, they may go direct to the original supplier.

Businesses that supply products over the Internet direct to consumers are often referred to as B2Cs (business to customer). Those that supply direct to other businesses are known as B2Bs (business to business).

Many other companies use the Internet as an additional outlet to supplement their normal methods of operation. Because they are already visible to their customers by their physical appearance in the high street or elsewhere, these operations are also known as "clicks and mortar." Click onto the BMW Website, for example, and you can see a whole range of cars without leaving your room.

SUPERMARKETS

In the late 1990 some of the larger supermarkets in the UK introduced systems to allow customers to set up an order through the Internet, with delivery to the customer's door. With these systems once a standard order is set up the customer can order the same items the following week or make changes as necessary, through the Internet.

Because the company has largely turned a self-service operation by the customer into a company provided service, this type of operation does incur increased costs and a small nominal charge is made to the customer to cover about half of these costs. In 2001, one of these supermarkets, Tesco, joined forces with US company, Safeway, to provide an Internet delivery service in the US. In the deal Safeway agreed to supply groceries from some of its 1535 stores in the US.

TRANSPORT AND TRAVEL

Many travel agents and tour operators, such as Thomas Cook and Tauck, have set up Websites, through which people can browse the latest offers and order holidays at special prices at virtually the last minute. Some airlines, too, such as Delta are seeking to move a significant proportion of their sales onto the Internet. In June 2001, they sold some 370,000 tickets online, a 50% increase in online sales over the same month in the previous year; they accounted for more than 8% of tickets sold.

For some other airlines, especially the new low cost airlines such as easyJet, online bookings are the norm. This method ensures that operations costs are kept to a minimum, thereby allowing flexibility on price to the customer. Eighty five per cent of easyJet's sales, for example, are made over the Internet. Many individual hotels and hotel chains, such as Hilton and Sheraton have their own Websites, through which bookings can be made direct.

Several of the larger airlines such as Singapore, Delta, American and United Airlines intend to offer their customers Internet access from their seats. How long will it be before we don't need to take holidays at all, but simply plug ourselves into a virtual reality device and visit wherever we want without leaving our own armchairs?

ESTATE AGENTS

Many estate agents offer the opportunity to view properties in detail through their Websites. They often offer several pictures of the property, allowing prospective purchasers to view different rooms and the garden. Some agents, like Chancellor's in the UK, even offer the option of a 360-degree look at some rooms and the garden. There are two great advantages here in that it:

» attracts a larger number of people to particular properties allowing an agent to meet with several prospective purchasers in one morning, thus cutting out unproductive traveling time; and
» allows those for whom the property is not suitable to recognize this at an early stage.

Operational effort is, therefore, focused on those who are most likely to want to buy the property.

AIR TRAFFIC CONTROL

It is not actually necessary to be able physically to see air traffic in order to control its movement. In fact, the new control center being built by the UK National Air Traffic Services (NATS) in south Hampshire is well removed from the current control center, which is in West Drayton near London Heathrow airport. In fact, with the introduction of new communications, air traffic could be controlled even more remotely than that. Were the political will there, the large number of national control centers throughout Europe could be rationalized into a much smaller number, bringing significant savings to the industry.

BANKING

Many banks, such as Barclays, for example, now offer customers the option of managing their own accounts. Using the Internet, customers can enter their accounts via a password and move money between their accounts, pay bills and set up direct debits. While this is very attractive for customers because they have direct access without having to go to their bank and wait in a queue, it is even more appealing for the company itself because, once the initial system is set up, the customer does the work. It has, therefore, turned the operation into a self-service operation.

CALL CENTERS

Call centers have been around for several years now, typically in the banking, retail and transport sectors, and the Internet has offered them the opportunity of providing a one stop center which can deal with all telephone and Internet communications. To handle the sheer volume of communications the centers are often very large. In many cases staff have to meet high performance levels and the work itself can often be rather routine, so there are often particular issues relating to staff motivation. We will look at an example of a call center in the case study later in this chapter.

OTHER OPPORTUNITIES

On a general note, applicable within any industry, the Internet has offered organizations other opportunities. Let's look at some in more detail.

Working from home

Depending upon the job they are doing, some staff can be allowed to work either partly or totally from home, communicating with the main office through the Internet. This can often result in an employee being more effective in that they can work away from office distractions. It may also allow the organization to share desks between workers (known as "hot-desking"), who agree to stagger the times they work from the office, thus saving on office space and furniture. The integrated US/UK utility company Powergen, provides hot-desking facilities for more than 300 of its 5000 UK based employees.

There are some possible disadvantages, however. Some find just as many distractions at home. Home working can also lead to an individual becoming isolated from the rest of their team and it is essential that they meet up at regular periods. The practice of hot-desking also brings its problems. Many workers feel that they do not belong anywhere and that they have no personal space of their own.

It is also possible that staff not able to work from home because of the nature of their job (at a front line counter interacting with customers, for example) may become dissatisfied because others are apparently enjoying a "perk" which is not available to them.

Unless these issues are addressed, the advantages of using home working can be outweighed by the disadvantages.

Absent staff can keep in touch

This is particularly useful in those operations where people have to travel regularly between sites. They can now keep in touch with all of the latest developments. They can also use what used to be considered down time (for example on a long flight) to file reports.

Simultaneous transmission

With the advent of e-mail, it is now possible for organizations with several sites, (including those which have offices and factories scattered throughout the world) to send advice of important issues simultaneously. In the travel industry, this might include updating fares information that needs to be done at the same time throughout all of the company's outlets. It would also be important in communicating vital policy changes, mergers or takeovers to staff throughout the organization at the same time.

EXERCISING CAUTION

While there are many advantages to the operations function as we have seen above, there are also some areas where caution needs to be exercised. These are mainly in the areas of:

Security

Clearly, it is most important that customers making purchases over the Internet are reassured that their credit card numbers and other personal documents cannot fall into the hands of people who might wish to use them for fraudulent purposes. Most companies overcome this by using secure channels. The US clothes manufacturer, Land's End, use their focus on security of information as a selling point in their marketing effort.

Quality

We saw in Chapters 2 and 3 how important quality is to the operations function. It is more difficult to put quality assurance systems into place if your products are being transferred direct from your supplier to your customer. The same applies if the operations process is handed over to the customers themselves.

Capacity

The very speed of e-mail communication means that people begin to equate its use with a quick response. Whereas, they might have expected to wait a week or even two for a response to a letter, they often expect a response to an e-mail within an hour. Yet, how many organizations are geared up to provide this sort of service? If an organization is not careful, it can find itself with a backlog of e-mail queries or orders, which act as a bottleneck to the rest of the operating system.

Let's now take a closer look at an organization that has adopted e-commerce as its main approach and is making a huge success out of it.

CASE STUDY: EGG

In October 1998, Prudential, the UK financial services company, set up a new company called Egg, initially offering savings, mortgages and loans. It describes itself as the UK's leading provider of online financial services. Egg's customers gain access via a range of channels including WAP mobile phones, interactive digital TV, the telephone and, of course, the Internet. The new company makes extensive use of the Internet and a large proportion of its staff support that medium.

Egg has three main call centers in the UK, in Derby, Dudley and London. The one at Derby, for example, is very large. There are 1,500 employees on the same floor, with an open plan arrangement, including the executive managers.

Egg go to a lot of trouble to ensure that the staff are motivated and happy in their work, which can often be a problem in call centers where a lot of the work can be relatively routine. Strategies include:

» dividing the large number of staff into small teams, many of them bearing a name or identity, supported by various signs, logos and mascots;
» appointing team leaders; and
» providing a whole range of relaxation facilities such as Mediterranean style breakout rooms, where staff can go to "chill out," have a cup of coffee, play pool, or just read a book. There is a TV room, a shop and a restaurant.

James Bell, head of customer relations at Egg explains: "Our focus is on the customer experience. They are at the heart of everything we do. Without them, there is no point in coming to work in the morning."

To ensure that quality standards are maintained by staff all customer communications such as phone calls and e-mails are recorded.

In March 2000, Egg launched the first investment supermarket in the UK, now providing access to over 266 investment funds from 24 of the leading fund providers over the Internet. Whilst it provides an execution only service, in that no financial advice is given, there is a lot of information available to the Egg customer who wants to learn more and make informed decisions.

Egg also offers tools to practice on before decisions are made. These include the "investor profiler" and the "virtual portfolio" where a customer can build a pretend portfolio of shares and investment funds and watch what happens to their investment; they can evaluate how they feel when their investment goes up or down and compare it to various indices before making a decision about whether to buy or not.

Clearly, as influential players in the financial services industry, Egg feels that it is their duty to educate the consumer. Education takes a very high profile in the organization for staff too. Indeed a "learning for all" culture is very evident. Apart from being at the forefront of e-commerce relationships with customers, Egg is making full use of the

World Wide Web for their staff. They have just launched their own "virtual university" called egglearn.com.

Staff have access to training and development from around the world using the Internet and also work towards qualifications. The service includes live, online, training courses as well as e-mail help facilities on any subject. Eventually, Egg hopes to offer this service to customers as well.

Staff in the centers also have access to the "mental gym" which is a type of open learning center. Here they can access, in a relaxed and beautifully decorated and furnished environment, computer based training programs, books and videos on both work-related subjects and a whole host of other topics.

Egg's effective use of e-communications in relation to both customers and its staff seems to work out well for the customer, because out of a population of around 60 million in the UK, Egg already have a customer base of approximately one million, which is growing daily.

KEY LEARNING POINTS

> The e-dimension has brought significant change to a wide range of industries.
> The e-dimension has involved the customer more closely in the operations process.
> The e-dimension allows communication with remote staff.
> The e-dimension allows costs to be reduced.

The Global Dimension

Explores the key issues facing organizations that want to operate globally, including:

» the key differences between operating globally and locally;
» the impact on the way in which operations are managed;
» the effects of culture;
» differences in technology;
» strategic partnerships; and
» case study: British Airways.

In this chapter we look at the opportunities the global marketplace offers to the operations function. Let's begin by looking at what changes might need to be made to the outputs of the process.

OUTPUTS

If an organization wants to produce the same product for several different markets, the first question it needs to ask is whether they need to be changed in any way to take account of cultural, geographical or climatic variations in different countries.

Those people who are responsible for marketing will usually be able to find this out by carrying out market research and looking at what competitors are doing. For example, when designing a truck for sale in one of the less developed countries where roads are in relatively poor condition, it may be necessary to strengthen the suspension system. In addition, any vehicle destined for an overseas market will need to have the driving wheel set on the appropriate side and meet any specific safety regulations that might be in operation in that country.

Coca Cola, for example, whose headquarters are in Atlanta, Georgia, USA, has local operations in nearly 200 countries worldwide. They "think local and act local, because we need to listen to all the voices around the world asking for beverages that span the entire spectrum of tastes and occasions."

In the construction industry, the same house might be built with air conditioning as standard in a country with a hot climate, and with a wood burning central heating system in a cold climate. In the entertainment world, some types of entertainment might have to be changed in some way; for example, many Western countries allow nudity in the theatre, but this would offend people in many other countries. If showing cinematic films in another country, the company may need to offer subtitles or dub translations onto the film.

Another output we need to consider is *waste*. The operations process may have a detrimental impact on the local environment, particularly with regard to waste products. This would be especially important if any dangerous waste were produced needing specialist companies to dispose of it. Production of waste is likely to lead to opposition and objections from the local community. If there is a possibility that the operation will have an impact on the wider issue of care for the environment or global warming, then there may even be international protests.

The importance of protecting the environment is recognized by the most successful organizations. McDonald's, for example, was awarded the Audubon Society's Golden Arches Award for Environmental Leadership in 2001 in recognition of their long record of significant contributions to conservation. This included the recycling, since 1990, of over a million tons of corrugated cardboard; McDonald's has also, during that time, purchased more than $3 billion worth of products made from recycled materials.

We will also be looking at Nestle's and Ford's environmental policies in Chapter 7.

Let's now consider the inputs into the system.

INPUTS

We saw, in Chapter 2, that there are three main types of inputs:

» materials (either raw or semi-finished);
» information (raw data or information); and
» the customer.

Materials

Some materials are unique. If a network of coffee outlets, for example, offered Colombian coffee on their menus, then the coffee beans will need to originate from Colombia.

If the materials are not unique, there are often many different places to obtain them. Where the organization obtains them and how they manage the supply may depend upon the following factors:

» Quantity – they may only be available locally in limited quantities.
» Quality – there may be better quality materials available elsewhere.
» Price – it may be cheaper to import from elsewhere, even allowing for transport costs.
» Local restrictions – there may be import quotas or other restrictions in place which means the materials must be obtained within the local country.
» Transport arrangements – if taking materials into the country, can reliable and economic transport arrangements be set up?

» Reliability of supply – unless a significant level of stocks are maintained, even a short break in the supply pipeline could bring the operation to a halt (we will look at stock/inventory in more detail in Chapter 6).

» Storage facilities – can imported materials be easily stored? If the country is hotter, what effect will this have on the materials? Will they need to be refrigerated? If it is colder, will they need to be kept warm? And will this increase the cost of production?

» Security of the materials – it may be necessary to take into account the level of crime locally.

In addition, the suitability of the materials used in the normal production processes will need to be considered. If there are significant differences in climate, will the product still work with the normal components? A camera might freeze, for example, in a very cold climate. Will its components stand up to desert sand storms or to prolonged periods of sunshine or rain? Similarly, if processing food, care will need to be taken to avoid ingredients that would be forbidden or offensive in a particular country.

Information (raw data or information)

As more and more advanced technology offers new ways of handling data, some of the key questions will focus around what stage the communications technology has · reached in the country concerned.

There may also be cultural issues concerning what information is or is not regularly gathered within a particular country. Journalists, for example, may find different attitudes to the privacy of individuals in different countries. Let's examine some of the key issues.

Availability

Is the information available in the overseas country in the format in which it is needed? For example, if the company produces statistics on spending patterns in the US or one of the more developed countries where customer surveys are commonplace, would the raw data be available in some other countries where this type of information has not been processed before? The company might have to set up its own system for gathering the data before it can start working on it.

Disseminating information

Satellite equipment and the Internet has made it much easier to move information around, even in countries where telecommunications are less advanced. Language barriers can be overcome by employing people who speak the local language or by ensuring that staff have the opportunity to learn.

Storage of information

Account must be taken of any additional regulations such as the Data Protection and Freedom of Information Acts which apply in Europe, the US and elsewhere. How secure is the information, both in respect of computerized and hard copy formats? Backup systems may also be needed in case of power failures.

Suitability of the information

Information may be available, but it may have a slightly different meaning in the culture of the country concerned. For example, data that shows the relative amounts of money spent on food and leisure pursuits may reflect a preference in one country but an economic necessity in another.

Now let's look at the third of the main inputs, the customer.

The customer

Every different country will have its own national culture or even several different cultures within it. What may be taken for granted in one country may not be so easy to apply in a different one. Here are some of the key issues that must be taken into account.

Restrictions

Some activities may be prohibited. For example, in Muslim countries, it may not be possible to sell alcohol in bars or restaurants. Similarly, if the customer would normally be touched during the process, as in hairdressing, this might not be appropriate in some cultures. Using local staff in the operations process will usually be a great help, as they can advise on these areas.

Transport

If the organization transports people around, passengers in some cultures will expect services to run punctually to a timetable. Others may expect the service to depart when it is full.

Hotels

Even tour operators find it difficult to classify hotels into a meaningful set of standards that could apply worldwide, and most set out their own. So, a hotel might be three star according to the local system in operation, but rated either two or four star by a tour operator who is focusing on a particular sector of clientele. Another tour operator might rate the hotel quite differently.

It is necessary, therefore, to be quite clear about the market for any hotel that might be planned, to ensure that the necessary facilities are provided to achieve the required rating. Some customers may have several different levels of expectations. At the Taj Hotel Group's Rambagh Palace Hotel, in Jaipur, India, people arrive from all over the world to enjoy the timeless, traditional ambience of the former Maharaja's palace; they are also glad to find the latest communications equipment, hot baths and fine dining.

OPERATIONAL ISSUES

We can now consider some of the issues involved in the operations process relating to:

» buildings;
» local infrastructure;
» plant and equipment;
» people; and
» suppliers.

Buildings and the operational site

Where, exactly, will they be located and what format will they take? Many countries, for example, have development areas in which companies are given grants if they move there. This was one of the considerations for Nissan, for example, when they set up their factory in the north-east of England. The local government is likely to insist that local jobs are created in return for any special grants or relaxation in business rates.

If the organization needs to convert any of the buildings or build new ones it needs to take into consideration any special restrictions that exist locally. For example, some countries only allow hotels to be built in two stories to preserve the natural beauty of the location. These include many of the islands of the Pacific Ocean, the Indian Ocean and the Caribbean, and other areas where tourism is a major industry. Others have set aside areas of outstanding beauty in which developments are restricted. There is currently a great debate in the US about how much development might be allowed in the state of Alaska.

Local infrastructure

What is the local infrastructure like, in terms of roads and rail and air networks? Will it make access easy to the operations area, for suppliers or customers? This was one of the very significant factors in Disney's choice of Paris as their European site, because it offers excellent access for visitors and suppliers alike.

The reliability of power supplies and telecommunications equipment may also be a factor.

Plant and machinery

The local running costs of a factory or premises are important. For example, it might be cheaper to locate the plant elsewhere, in an adjacent country, if power, fuel or labor is less expensive there. In the year 2000, several haulage companies moved their operational base from the UK to France in response to the high fuel and road tax charges that were prevalent in the UK.

Another major factor will be the availability of the technology that is needed and the staff to operate it.

People

Perhaps the first factor to consider is who will manage the plant. Will the organization appoint one of its own managers or appoint someone local? There are other questions to consider:

» Can a large enough skilled workforce be recruited locally to carry out the operations?
» Will local staff have the knowledge and ability to operate the technology being used?
» Will a local workforce be content, willing, or able to follow the current systems and procedures?
» Will they need to be trained by the organization's own staff, at least in the initial stages of the operation until knowledge and skills can be cascaded?
» If the company does send its own trainers out, how long are they likely to be needed and what support will be provided for them and their dependents while they are there?

Employing local staff might be a particularly good selling point for the products, because it will show that the company is in tune with the local people.

Fons Trompenaars, in his book *Riding the Waves of Culture* (1993)[1], has studied the ways in which different cultures react to each other in various situations. He suggests that it is important to understand the different ways in which people:

» manage and conceive of time (tradition may be more or less important than progress);
» regard status (age may confer status automatically or status may come with the job);
» relate to each other (some cultures are outgoing, while others are more reserved);
» relate to the organization (some see it as a family group of which they are part, others see it as a place to stand out from the crowd);
» respond to rules (some will go their own ways despite what organizational policy sets out); and
» view their relationship with nature (some feel they have full control over their lives, others that they must accept what happens).

Local employees are likely to have a greater understanding of the language, culture and customs of their colleagues and of their local customers. This might be especially important in service industries where the customer is being transformed, such as the hotel or transport industries.

Several countries have a minimum wage level. The EU, for example, requires member countries to set out a minimum hourly wage. There is, therefore, the possibility that the cost of local labor might be so high that it is more economic to manufacture a product somewhere else and bring it into the country for sale in its finished state. This factor would need to be weighed against the other factors mentioned above which suggest that employing local people would be more advantageous.

Suppliers

Key factors when choosing suppliers in the global marketplace include the following:

» Where are they located?
» Is the supply route acceptable?
» Can they meet the schedules?
» How competitive are their prices?
» What is their attitude to quality?
» Will local holidays affect supplies?

With current technology, a company based in one country can very easily use staff in another country to process information. We will see in the case study later in this chapter that British Airways processes some of its information and communications in India, where the operation can be carried out effectively at a lower cost than it could be in the UK.

On the manufacturing side, it is quite usual for clothes to be made in Taiwan and China, where operating costs are relatively lower, on behalf of companies operating in Europe and the US.

FINANCE AND PARTNERSHIPS

Two further factors that need to be considered are the financial aspects, and the degree to which strategic alliances or partnerships can be effective in operating globally.

Finance

It will be very important that money can be moved easily into and out of the country. Thought needs to be given to which currencies the organization will be working in. Can it easily exchange the currency, for example, and how much will it cost to do so?

In some countries, local currencies are not convertible and profits cannot, therefore, be taken out of the country. In others, there may be more than one currency that is in routine usage. In Mexico the peso and US dollar are accepted; in the US and Canada, American and Canadian dollars are accepted; while the euro has been introduced in some countries in the EU and will be replacing some national currencies. It is likely that many businesses in the UK, which has not yet embraced the euro and has retained the pound sterling, will accept euro coins and notes from the early part of 2002, when they are introduced in the rest of the EU.

Partnerships

Over the last 20 years, as organizations have begun to take a more global approach, many have found it to be more effective to work in partnership with other companies to carry out their global operation.

Rather than provide a service itself or produce a manufactured product, it can be very effective for an organization to join with another partner who is already providing it. This can either be in the form of a takeover or merger, or through a formal alliance in which companies agree to work together and share the profits.

The latter is very prevalent in the airline industry. Many airlines collaborate to offer their customers a wider choice of destinations, without actually having to provide the service themselves. Thus, passengers of one airline can travel to destinations offered by another airline, buying only one through-ticket and without having to handle their luggage en route.

Partnerships also allow airlines to share the costs of flying a particular route, with each airline providing a share of the flights and customers being able to use any of the flights, whichever airline they booked through. These arrangements are usually referred to as code shares, because the airplane will carry the flight number of both partners. British Airways, for example, has a code share arrangement with both

American Airlines and Qantas. However, there are also some full-blown alliances such as:

» Star Alliance, made up of 15 members: Air Canada, Air New Zealand, ANA, Ansett Australian, Austrian Airlines, bmi British Midland, Lauda, Lufthansa, Mexicana, Scandinavian, Singapore, Thai, Tyrolean, United and Varig (Brazil); and
» Oneworld Alliance, made up of eight members: British Airways, American Airlines, Qantas, Cathay Pacific, Finnair, Iberia, LanChile and Aer Lingus.

They are becoming very powerful forces in the industry, offering their member companies increased sales and reduced costs, and it is likely that more alliances will occur in the future.

In other cases, airlines have merged. In March 2000, Singapore Airlines, for example, bought a 49% share of Virgin Atlantic in order to give themselves the capability of entering the US market.

On the manufacturing side, it is normal for large and complex projects to be spread over a large number of companies and countries. For example, the airplane manufacturer, Airbus, is owned by BAE Systems of the UK and the European Aeronautic Defence and Space Company (EADS), which is itself formed from a merger of Aerospatiale – Matra of France, Daimler Chrysler Aerospace of Germany and CASA of Spain. The various Airbus models are manufactured throughout Europe at various sites. Each produces a section of the aircraft, which is then assembled at the final assembly lines in Toulouse in France and in Hamburg in Germany. The company makes use of over 1500 different suppliers throughout the world.

The US based Starbucks Coffee Company has a Swiss partner in Bon Appetit Group AG, with whom they have opened a number of stores in Switzerland and are currently making plans to enter the Austrian market, in Vienna, at the end of 2001.

In each case, the collaborative approach represents the companies' desire to find the optimum way to carry out each part of the operation taking all of the operational issues into account.

Let's now consider a success story as far as carrying out global operations is concerned.

CASE STUDY: BRITISH AIRWAYS

In 1997 British Airways issued a new mission statement that proclaimed that it wanted to be the "undisputed leader in world travel." This was a change from their former mission, which was related specifically to their activities as an airline. One of their stated goals was to have a "global network and a global outlook."

We can look at the network first, which can be said to be truly global, due to the company's partnerships with other airlines. It is part of the Oneworld Alliance as mentioned earlier in this chapter. This gives them access to destinations far beyond their former confines. While they do serve directly a number of gateway cities in the United States, they can now access a huge range of destinations in the North American market through their partnership with American Airlines, with whom they also have a code share.

Similarly, their alliance with Iberia and with LanChile gives access to a large number of destinations in South America. Finnair increases the Scandinavian opportunities. Cathay Pacific and Qantas allow access into the Far East, Australasia and the South Pacific. Aer Lingus offers additional European options.

In addition to offering new destinations, the Oneworld Alliance, through also selling each other's services, can find economies of scale in their selling costs. The specific code share arrangements with American Airlines and Qantas mean that British Airways passengers have an increased frequency of flights to the key North American and Australian cities, which British Airways serves directly, while the company does not have to put on any extra services. The alliance has also allowed British Airways to withdraw direct services to some cities such as Auckland, New Zealand and to Melbourne, Australia, with passengers utilizing Qantas or Cathay Pacific services instead. This significantly reduces costs.

The company was very quick to see the value of employing local cabin crew on their services to areas of the world where the culture and language are significantly different. They employ local cabin crew on services to and from Japan, India, Pakistan, Bangladesh and South America, as well as many other worldwide and European destinations. They also encourage their cabin crews to have a second language. Menus reflect the tastes of their destinations too.

Two other aspects are worth mentioning concerning the introduction of new technology, which we talked about in Chapter 4:

Call flow

The company uses sophisticated telecommunications technology allowing it to switch incoming telephone calls between various call centers at New York and Houston in the US and at Glasgow, Newcastle and Manchester in the UK. By using a call flow control when one call center becomes overloaded calls can be switched to another where capacity is available. This allows effective management of resources, ensuring that the company is in line with the number of calls received.

Work flow

Current technology allows organizations to send work via e-mail to other countries to have it completed where costs are cheaper. Some of British Airways' administrative work is sent via e-mail from the US and UK to staff in India where operating costs are lower. It is processed by staff in Delhi and then sent back to the originating location for further action as necessary.

As we can see, British Airways takes a global approach to their operations.

KEY LEARNING POINTS

» Globalization has made the marketplace more competitive.
» Globalization offers more choices in managing operations.
» With greater choice comes greater complexity.
» Partnerships and alliances can allow costs to be shared and reduced.
» Local staff can play an important part in global operations.

NOTES

1 Trompenaars, F. (1993) *Riding the Waves of Culture*, Economist Books, London.

Operations: The State of the Art

Examines the key debates, including:

» When is a product not a product?
» Which operating system?
» Fixed capacity or flexible capacity?
» Push or pull?
» Costs or quality?
» The environment – are you friend or foe?

In this section we can examine some of the key operational decisions in more detail. We will consider the following:

» When is a product not a product?
» Which operating system?
» Fixed capacity or flexible capacity?
» Push or pull?
» Costs or quality?
» The environment – are you friend or foe?

WHEN IS A PRODUCT NOT A PRODUCT?

Answer – when it's a service? Well, it's not that simple.

Usually, when we talk about products, we can be referring to either goods products, that is manufactured products, or service products. In most cases, any of the concepts can be applied to either type of product. However, there are a few distinctions that are often made between the attributes of the two and which can be important to the operations function.

In most cases, although a particular attribute may be more common in a service or in a goods product, the attributes can be found in either. The key point for people involved in the operations function is to identify the attributes that each of their products has and manage production with these in mind. Let's identify some of the key attributes here.

Tangibility – goods products tend to be tangible, while service products are not. You can't touch or see service products, though you can see the results. No travelers ever see the air traffic control service, for example, but we see the airplanes take off and land safely. We can also see and touch the clean garment we collect from the laundry.

Interactivity – services involve interaction with the customer. They usually need the customer to take part in some way; for example, they will eat a meal in a restaurant. Goods products can be manufactured without the customer being involved; it is, though, becoming more and more common, especially in large manufacturing projects, for customers to be involved in the design process and in the quality monitoring as the project moves forward.

Simultaneousness – the service will usually be offered when the customer is there, while goods can be prepared beforehand (though our example above regarding laundering which is carried out behind the scenes proves that there are exceptions to any rule).

Perishability – services have a sell-by date. Once an empty seat on a bus or airplane has left its departure point, it is lost forever. Similarly, if a tour operator does not sell a particular two-week summer holiday, it too is lost. Many goods, of course, are perishable too, especially food products.

Consistent quality – goods can be produced to a consistent quality while services tend to be delivered inconsistently. A factory machine can produce any number of identical goods one after another (though statistical process control will actually suggest that there may still be infinitesimal differences in each product), while a service may be delivered by different people on behalf of different people, so it will be difficult for any two deliveries to be exactly the same. If a customer reacts in a particular way, then the person delivering the service may adjust the service to take account of this.

Front line – services are usually delivered direct to the customer, either by telephone or face to face (though more and more through the Internet, of course, as we have seen in Chapter 4). This means that the person delivering it is in the front line and will be first to receive a complaint from the customer if there is something wrong. The producer of a goods product will not usually be the first person to hear the customer's complaint.

We can identify processes as being either front office (interacting with the customer) or back room (hidden from the customer). The organization needs to have a policy on how much they want the customer to be able to see. It has become rather trendy in some restaurants to allow customers to see through into the kitchen.

Clearly, the more staff interfacing directly with the customer, the more people there will be who need to be trained in interpersonal skills. Some organizations prefer to give the impression that they operate with few staff to keep costs, and therefore, prices, down; most of their people will be back room. Some of the quality cruise lines, on the other hand, offer their large numbers of staff as a unique selling point to demonstrate how much they cosset their customers.

As mentioned above, it is important that each of the products is analyzed to identify which of the attributes apply, irrespective of whether it is a goods or service product. It should also be noted that most operations processes result in both a goods and service product. For example, a supermarket may sell a tin of beans, which is a service; however, it will have been produced in a manufacturing process earlier. Similarly, a company might produce nuts and bolts that are goods products, but when they deliver them to the customer they are providing a service.

WHICH OPERATING SYSTEM?

There are five main types of operating system:

» project;
» jobbing;
» batch;
» line; and
» continuous.

As Table 6.1 shows each will be appropriate for certain levels of volume or variety.

Table 6.1 Appropriate operating systems for different levels of volume and variety.

Low volume/ high variety	Medium volume/ medium variety	High volume/ low variety
Project Jobbing	Batch	Line Continuous

Project

Project systems can be used for a very high variety of products. They are usually made up of a number of interrelated activities focusing upon accomplishing a particular task and are a one off. The American and Soviet space programs and, currently, The Three Gorges Dam in China are examples of huge and complex projects being implemented over a period of several years, though many projects are far less complex and may take weeks or even days.

There are a number of very useful tools that can be used to help people manage projects, which are usually placed under the control of a designated project manager:

» Gantt charts (designed by Henry Gantt in 1917), which allow activities to be plotted against time on a chart, identifying when each specific activity should begin and end, though they don't show any links or relationships between activities.
» Network analysis, which identifies events and activities and plots them on a diagram, showing how long each activity will take and its relationship with other events and activities.

There is a more detailed explanation of Gantt charts and network analysis in Chapter 8.

Jobbing

Like projects systems, jobbing can be used for a high variety of products. They, too, are tailored specifically for a particular task, though they will be far less complex and they will be produced in greater quantity. Jobbing systems will typically involve only one or two people at a time, who will carry out a particular job and then move swiftly on to another, which may be in the same field, but which will be different in some way from the previous one. Freelance writers of training materials, for example, will spend time writing a set of materials for one company and then may go on quickly to write a different set for another company.

Similarly, landscape gardeners will work on one particular garden then move on to another which will present them with a related, but different, set of activities. People involved in jobbing will also find Gantt charts useful, especially if they are working on more than one job at a time and they can plot which activity they should be doing on a particular day/part day.

If the garden was very large and required a complex design, with several suppliers and designers becoming involved over a longer period of time, with each relying on a particular task being completed before they could carry out theirs, it could be regarded as a project and a network analysis would be useful.

Batch

Batch systems are used for small to medium quantities with lower levels of variety and are likely to be used where there is a range of similar products of different shapes or sizes, such as tools, fastenings, clothes and food products. In services, they may be used for sending out invoices or paying bills; organizations often refer to "the check run at the end of the month."

Typically, a machine will be set up to produce a batch of products that will be the same. The machine can then be reset to produce another set of products to a different specification. Advantages of the process include the ability to produce a large number of items relatively quickly. The disadvantages include the fact that if a particular customer wants a small number of several items, the company will need to choose between:

» producing a small run of each item, accepting the down time while machines are reset for each run; and
» producing larger quantities of each item and storing the surplus.

Line

Line systems are used when large volumes are being produced of a very small variety of products. We saw, in Chapter 5, that Airbus assemble their airplanes at assembly plants in Toulouse and Hamburg. A typical assembly line will be set up for one main product (though there may be differing versions of it which may have different assembly lines) and the various parts of the product will be assembled in turn as it moves down the line. White goods (such as refrigerators and washing machines), autos and airplanes are particularly associated with this system. Many of the inputs into a line system will themselves have been produced in a batch or another line system.

Continuous

Continuous systems are used for very high volumes of little variety; thus they are used by companies like Shell and BP in gas and oil pipelines where they flow continuously. In services, the electricity power grid and air traffic control could be considered as continuous systems.

FIXED CAPACITY OR FLEXIBLE CAPACITY?

Capacity can be defined as the amount of product produced in a given time. So, it could be expressed as 3000 articles per month or 36,000 articles per year. Airports, for example, expect their air traffic control suppliers to achieve so many take-offs and landings per hour. On this count, Chicago's O'Hare Airport is generally reckoned to be the world's busiest airport overall. Capacity planning falls into three main areas:

» long term (called aggregate planning) sets out the fixed assets;
» medium term – identifies strategies to deal with fluctuations in demand; and
» short term/immediate – deals with exceptional items or emergencies.

Different approaches are needed for each.

Long-term planning

How far an organization plans ahead will depend upon:

» the type of business it is in;
» the life cycle of its products; and
» how much flexibility is needed.

An airplane manufacturing company like Boeing in the US or Airbus in Europe, will look at least 10 years ahead, probably longer. A manufacturer of novelty Christmas toys might look only as far ahead as the end of the year.

Whichever applies, decisions must be made about the size and location of the operation and the amount of fixed resources that will be needed, such as buildings, plant and machinery, operating system, staff and storage space. Another key decision is whether to work shifts (three shifts treble the capacity of one shift and also make use of machines that would otherwise be idle). These decisions will depend upon the likely demand in the immediate future and upon whether the organization:

» makes everything itself or buys some or even all items in from suppliers;
» stores its products or produces them only when they have an order; and
» expects there to be significant growth in demand in the longer term, leading to the need for expansion of the operation.

If there is likely to be growth in demand, it will have to consider at the outset whether it should buy or lease additional land, building space or other long-term resources so that it can grow into it.

We also saw, in Chapter 5, another way of coping with long-term increases in demand, which is to find a partner who can handle some of the capacity.

A crucial question is whether to plan for minimum, average or maximum capacity. If resources are set up for the maximum, there may be long periods when the operation is producing a lot less than it is capable of doing and it will still be incurring most of the running costs (staff, power, rates, rent), so it will be inefficient. This will also be the least flexible approach, since, if the organization decides to change strategy, it may be locked into payments for rent, machinery and staff for a relatively long period and it may be expensive to make those changes.

If capacity is set at the minimum, the operation will be working flat out and will be unable to meet demand most of the time; it will also be very vulnerable to a breakdown of machinery or a shortage of supplies. Although this may, at first sight, appear to be the most flexible approach (since the organization has committed the least amount of resources), in fact, it is likely to spend so much time reacting to problems and late deliveries that there may be no time to plan significant change.

Setting capacity somewhere in the middle allows the plant to operate at an economic level, with medium-term strategies for managing the upward and downward fluctuations in demand. This approach should also leave time to plan future strategy in a considered and analytical way and, combined with the medium- and short-term strategies outlined below can provide a very flexible approach.

Whichever approach is chosen, it is important to ensure that all parts of the operation are working towards the same capacity target; if they are not, the result will be a bottleneck.

Bottlenecks

A bottleneck can be described as a point that cannot cope with the inputs and resources that are trying to flow through it. At best, it will slow the whole system down to its own capability level and, at worst, it will cause a backlog that may threaten the integrity of the whole system. This applies as much to service industries as to manufacturing; if a call center cannot cope with the influx of telephone calls, a backlog of calls will grow and grow until, eventually, customers simply hear the engaged tone and take their business elsewhere.

Let's now consider some of the medium-term strategies that can be used in conjunction with the long-term planning described above.

Medium-term

There are a number of medium-term strategies that are available to ensure that the operating system works effectively. It is possible to address either the *demand* or the *supply*.

Demand

Differential pricing – charging more for a product at peak times and less at quiet times is a long proven method of manipulating demand. Telephone companies do it according to times of the day; tour operators do it according to the time of the year; airlines do it according to how late a flight is booked before departure.

Change the product into something else – this applies particularly to seasonal products such as fresh fruit, meat and fish where the excess fruit can be turned into jam and stored and sold later. Canning, salting and smoking meat and fish, and processing cheese also stimulate further demand for the product.

Supply

Smoothing – applies to manufactured products which are non perishable; a product continues to be made during periods of relatively quiet demand and it is stored for future use when demand outstrips production capacity

Queuing – is a very common method in many organizations. Hospital waiting lists are queues; call centers keep people queuing on the telephone, shops let people queue physically at the counter; airplanes queue in the sky for landing slots

Sub-contracting – some tasks are given to sub-contractors when demand is high, and are taken back into the organization when demand lessens.

Part time/flexible staff – in this way, the number of staff on duty can be increased at particular times of the day when demand may be at its peak.

Now that the operation is matching demand with capacity, through the application of the long- and short-term strategies that we have identified above, there needs to be a system for changing things at the last moment or at short notice to deal with unplanned emergencies, last minute orders or last minute cancellations. These changes will normally be managed by junior managers or supervisors, through, for example:

» working overtime;
» working on days off;
» changing schedules;
» hiring in an extra machine;
» hiring additional vehicles; and
» making hotel reservations for stranded passengers.

Delegating these decisions to front line managers will ensure that the organization is working effectively and economically at all times.

PUSH OR PULL?

In the UK, organizations refer to stock control, while US companies talk about inventory. Whatever it is called, there are significant costs incurred by keeping a large stock/inventory, and most organizations will focus a lot of time and effort to try to reduce the levels that they maintain. Do we *push* materials through the system or do we *pull* them through from the other end?

Stock can take many forms and it can be seen from Table 6.2 that there are some good reasons why it might be held.

There are, however, a number of costs that result from keeping high levels of stock:

Table 6.2 Reasons for holding stock.

Raw materials ready for input	Ensures a consistent supply
	Bulk purchase discounts can be obtained
	Buying can be completed in advance of a price increase
	Scarce resources, including seasonal goods can be bought
Partly finished goods (work in progress)	Allows the organization to work on different parts of the operation at the same time
Finished goods awaiting collection	Customers can see the products and can purchase immediately
	Provides an average supply of goods for sale
	Can provide against a breakdown in the production process
	Can help meet seasonal demand
Administrative items such as stationery	Keeps administrative systems going
Maintenance items and spares	Prevent breakdowns of plant and machinery
	Restore breakdowns if they occur

» warehouse rents;
» storage costs (such as racks and bays);
» handling costs;
» wastage (because so many items are available);
» damage;
» insurance;
» management time;
» deterioration and obsolescence (and possibly disposal costs); and
» financial opportunity costs.

Therefore, most organizations have strategies in place to reduce (or, in some cases, eliminate altogether) the amount of stock/inventory they hold. There are two main approaches:

» push systems; and
» pull systems.

Push systems

In push systems, a planned capacity level is set and a target of finished products, per week, or per month, is set. For each product a "bill of materials" will be identified, which is a list of the product split into its component parts.

Thus, if a chair is made up of four legs, a seat and a back, we can work out exactly how many of each we need for any given volume of chairs, because the volume we need for each is directly dependent on the volume of chairs. For 100 chairs, we know that we need 100 backs, 100 seats and 400 legs. These are usually referred to as dependent items, because the number needed is directly dependent on the number of finished products.

Each of the component parts will have to be supplied either from within the company or from a supplier; each will have a "lead time," which can be defined as the length of time between order and availability for use. Any operations system needs to build in all of the lead times to ensure that each item is ordered at the appropriate time. Traditionally, this has meant carrying an additional safety (or buffer) stock of each item, so that, if a delivery is late or the supply breaks down, the operations process will not be stopped.

The problem is that, if the company keeps safety stock for each item, the more different parts there are, the more stock it has to keep, which provides a strong argument for standardizing as many of the parts as possible.

There are sophisticated computer systems used in complex organizations to keep the various parts flowing in their correct quantities through the system. The systems are known as MRP I, and MRP II. They work out what parts need to be ordered at what time and initiate the orders. MRP II has an additional capability in that it usually integrates the financial systems of handling invoices and sending accounts and providing financial information. The final products are stored ready for collection by/delivery to customers or to be moved to sales outlets.

A key factor in push systems is that, in the event of a breakdown of equipment or supply, there will be a stock of finished products available for the customer.

Pull systems

Pull systems are usually known as just-in-time. They require a stable and predictable level of demand. The demand is agreed with customers and is divided into a daily total so that the same number of items is manufactured each day. The process is divided into several stages and each stage will only produce enough to satisfy demand in the next stage. The final products are collected by customers or delivered without being stored. Thus, stock is being pulled through the system.

Each workstation has a restricted number of containers in which parts are held. As it uses the parts and empties the containers, the containers are sent back to be refilled; thus a constant level of production is achieved and the workstation never has more parts than it needs.

At the very beginning of the process, external suppliers will also deliver containers (exactly enough for the next stage of the process) on a regular basis throughout the day. Thus, the company keeps no stock of raw materials or finished goods and the only materials it will have are those involved in the work in progress. It should be noted that the supplier will have no store of finished stocks either, as they only produce enough to satisfy each of their deliveries.

If there is a breakdown at any stage the containers would cease to move between the work stations because parts would not be being used. This would mean that all of the production would be stopped in a very short time, because work stations in advance of the breakdown would receive no further parts, while stations behind the breakdown would not be able to send any work forward. A breakdown would also result in the suppliers being stopped, so it is usual for companies and suppliers to work very closely together to foresee and prevent problems before they arise.

Unlike push systems, if there is a breakdown, there are no finished stocks available for the customer. This means that any problems that do occur have to be rectified very quickly. It calls for a real focus on quality at every stage of the system and just-in-time is usually carried out under a TQM approach, which we will look at later in this chapter.

The Japanese car manufacturer, Toyota, was one of the great pioneers of just-in-time, followed later by Nissan.

Just-in-time systems are not only found in manufacturing. Many service companies carry no stock. A magazine publisher, for example, can store the magazine electronically on its printing supplier's equipment. When it receives orders, it can simply ask the printer to produce the appropriate number of copies and send them off direct to the customer. In this case, the company holds no stock of either raw materials or finished goods.

Whichever approach an organization takes, it will also need to have a system for controlling materials used in the production process, but whose required numbers are not directly linked to the number of finished goods. If the chairs mentioned earlier were glued and varnished, it would not be so easy to work out exactly how much glue and varnish were needed for the production of our 100 chairs. Similarly, a fast food restaurant might know exactly how many sausages it needs for 30 sausage sandwiches; but how much brown or tomato sauce should they order? In a manufacturing situation, oil will be needed to keep machinery running freely. The printing company may need ink and other consumables. These are known as independent items.

Independent items

For independent items a safety or buffer stock is usually maintained. This is the amount of stock that is needed to ensure that the supply never runs out. The level of safety stock held will depend upon the average usage of the item and the lead time from ordering it and it being available for use. The more important the item is to the operation, the more precisely the level of safety stock will need to be calculated.

There are two other specific tools recognized as being particularly useful in controlling independent items:

» *Economic order quantity* – which identifies the most efficient quantities in which an item should be ordered; and
» *Pareto/ABC analysis* – which lets the organization set up an effective method of controlling the various items that it stocks.

Both of these are explained in more detail in Chapter 8.

One further point about stock/inventory control is the need to maintain spares for maintaining machines and equipment. Now that there are very high quality delivery organizations such as DHL and

Federal Express that will deliver next day, even same day, both locally, and internationally, there is often no need for a company to keep as many spares as it used to in the past. Lead times have often dropped to hours where they used to be measured in days or even weeks. Usually, the cost of transporting the spare is cheaper than the cost of storing it. Of course, items that are vital to a production line may need to be stocked anyway, especially in just-in-time systems where a breakdown could halt the whole process.

COSTS OR QUALITY?

Philip Crosby pioneered an approach (zero defects) arguing that it is less expensive to strive for quality than it is to tolerate low quality. The costs associated with high quality are:

» higher quality materials and other inputs may be more expensive;
» quality assurance systems need to be set up;
» staff need investment to improve their skills;
» getting things right first time requires the operating system to be designed and implemented to achieve the necessary attention to detail; and
» preventative maintenance of machines needs a planned program of down time (in the transport industry effective preventative mainte-nance is essential to ensure safety).

However, the costs associated with low quality may be even higher.

» Getting things wrong first time leads to wasted materials as the product may have to be produced again. It also leads to wasted machine and people hours during the rework and also in finding solutions as to why it went wrong and how it can be put right. In some instances, especially where there are safety implications, failure can be catastrophic
» Allowing machinery to break down leads to additional repair costs, more down time (which is unplanned and may be very incon-venient) and possible lost orders. In just-in-time systems, it may bring the whole workplace to a standstill as well as customers and suppliers.

» Allowing a sub standard product to reach the customer leads to:
  » complaints and possible loss of future revenue;
  » refunds of money;
  » loss of reputation;
  » additional delivery costs;
  » after sales repair work or replacement; and
  » in the worst cases, compensation when the sub standard product leads to other problems.

So, producing low quality products can be very expensive indeed.

We saw, in the analysis of the evolution of operations in Chapter 3, that there were many different initiatives by a number of consultants and theorists which have resulted in a composite approach now referred to as Total Quality Management. Here are some of the key characteristics of a TQM approach, which follow most of the points in Dr Edwards Deming's 14-point plan, which is usually regarded as a blueprint for the TQM approach and which can be found in Chapter 8.

Everyone in the organization is involved in the quality process - it is important that any TQM approach is fully supported by the highest level of management. The approach must also permeate right through the organization with everyone feeling that quality is their very own responsibility. Each person builds quality into their own particular part of the operation.

Usually, the organization will treat people within the organization as internal customers or suppliers whenever they are interacting with each other. The final customer who receives the product is then the external customer. The organization will also recognize other stakeholders who are affected by the organization in any way, such as:

» its suppliers;
» its shareholders;
» people who live nearby; and
» the environment.

Kaoru Ishikawa was a great believer in quality circles, which involve a team of people from different aspects of the organization analyzing specific issues and finding solutions. He also created the cause and effect diagram, which is still used as a technique in problem solving, and this can be viewed in more detail in Chapter 8.

A good example of an organization that uses quality circles is at Raffles Hotel in Singapore, which is world-renowned for its approach to quality. Here, they are called service focus groups; they are cross-functional so that any problem can be seen from all perspectives and they meet every week.

Set quality standards – in his 14–point plan Deming suggests that there are other measures of quality than the amount produced. It is important that people in the organization know what they are expected to produce. This may be especially important with service products as people may approach their delivery in slightly different ways; this will be exaggerated if they have no standards to which they can work. Examples of standards are:

» size (of a nut or a bolt);
» strength (of toughened glass);
» time within which (response to an e-mail);
» time without failure (an engine);
» quantity (a full pint in a beer glass);
» appearance (the right color);
» taste (of a meal in a restaurant); and
» on time (transport).

Work closely with suppliers – suppliers may be able to make suggestions as to how operations processes can be improved; in a TQM approach, an organization will tend to use tried and trusted suppliers upon whom they can rely and with whom they can work together to find improvements.

Prevention is better than cure – preventative maintenance to stop machinery breaking down is much better than allowing it to break down and then having to fix it. Building quality into the product is better than mending it later.

It's easier to get simple things right – there is the question of standardization versus variety and simplicity versus complexity. Providing greater variety may allow the company to satisfy a greater number of customer needs. However, the simpler the operation is and the less variety it has, the easier it is to get it right consistently over a period of time. There may well be good marketing reasons why variety is needed, but the company does need to be aware of the implications. It needs to use the appropriate operating system set up so that it can be sure of producing the products to a consistent quality.

We will see a case study in Chapter 7, which shows how an organization has made a very high reputation for itself by keeping things simple and how other companies in the same industry have seen the value of reducing the complexity of their operations.

Process control rather than acceptance sampling – it is better to monitor the quality of a product while it is being produced than waiting until the customer receives it, checks it and then rejects it. All organizations that follow a TQM approach have quality assurance systems built in to their processes.

Search for continuous improvement and innovation – this is what Tom Peters was referring to in his quote at the beginning of this book. As new technology keeps being invented, there will always be new ways of doing things and an organization needs to be constantly on the look out for them; we will see an example of innovation by Nissan in the case study in Chapter 7.

Search for solutions rather than blame – if an organization is to move forward and continuously improve, there may be a need to take some risks. Tom Peters said "fail forward." If things don't work out as well as expected, then seek a collaborative approach to find out how it can be made to work next time, rather than seeking to apportion blame by finding out whose fault it was and holding them up as a scapegoat. Apportioning blame will act as a barrier to continuous improvement.

Train and develop staff – if staff are fully trained and are allowed opportunities to develop their skills, they will be anxious to use them on the organization's behalf and will be likely to reward the organization by going that extra mile to do a good job. Many organizations are keen to meet international standards to show that they are developing their systems and their staff; in the UK, these include ISO 9000 and Investors in People.

In the US, McDonald's have their own "hamburger university," at Oak Brook, Illinois, where the company teaches staff the basics of its operations.

Use quality materials that are fit for the purpose – Joseph Juran championed the need for products to be "fit for use." Thus a garden spade should not crumple on the first occasion the user tries to put it into the ground. Durable materials in the spade's construction will allow it to be used to full potential over a reasonable lifetime.

A total quality approach may not be right for every organization as it will depend on a number of factors such as its size, the industry it is in and the environment in which it is operating as well as many other factors. However, most successful organizations will follow some of the approaches mentioned above.

THE ENVIRONMENT—ARE YOU FRIEND OR FOE?

There is no doubt that any organization that wishes to operate in today's society will have to ensure that it discharges all of its responsibilities towards the environment. In this broad term we can also include the health and safety of people with whom the organization comes into contact. There are three main reasons:

» the cost of safety, both in human and monetary terms, is usually much less than the cost of an accident;
» there are a whole range of laws that apply in different ways throughout the world, for whose transgressing there will be serious repercussions and serious penalties; and
» the attitude that people now have towards issues such as safety and the environment means that an organization is unlikely to be welcomed in any location if they are seen not to be fully aware in these matters.

In fact, being environmentally aware is becoming very much a plus factor from the marketing point of view and organizations have begun to use their attitudes towards the environment as part of their marketing effort. It is noticeable that many large and successful organizations, especially those who consider themselves to be global in nature, are taking a keen interest in projecting their image as environmentally friendly and safety aware. In Chapter 7 we will see a case study which looks at two very large and famous organizations who clearly take these matters very seriously and are using their response as a means of gaining competitive advantage.

Just as some organizations used the international management standards ISO 9000 as a badge to show how effective their management systems are, so now they are applying the new environmental standard ISO 14000 to show off their environmental credentials. This requires organizations to:

» give a top level commitment to environmental management;
» establish environmental objectives;
» put in place a program to meet the objectives; and
» review their performance against their objectives.

KEY LEARNING POINTS

» Goods and service products have a variety of different attributes.
» There is a range of operating systems available.
» There are a number of ways of managing capacity.
» Push systems maintain higher stock levels, though are at less risk from a breakdown.
» Pull systems maintain fewer stocks but are at a higher risk in case of a breakdown.
» Quality systems should be in place to ensure the operations process flows smoothly and that products meet customer requirements.
» Quality does not have to mean an increase in costs.
» Environmental concerns must be taken into account.

Operations Success Stories

Explains how Nissan, easyJet, Ford and Nestle have applied some of the operations concepts and introduced new technology to achieve success. It includes:

» a case study of Nissan's revival plan;
» a case study of easyJet's focus on keeping things simple; and
» a case study of Ford and Nestle's approach to the environment.

In this chapter we will be looking at three main case studies, each dealing with a slightly different aspect of operations. We will look at:

» Nissan's rationalization of their operating processes;
» easyJet's low cost approach to operations; and
» Ford and Nestle's approach to operations and their interaction with the environment.

Let's first look at Nissan.

CASE STUDY: NISSAN

At the end of the 1990s the Japanese car manufacturer, Nissan Motor Co., despite its excellent reputation for producing high quality, fuel efficient cars was not making a profit. In 1999, therefore, it made some significant operating decisions including:

» in March, creating an alliance with Renault, the French car manufacturer, giving the partners 9.1% of the world market for passenger cars, making them the sixth most important in the world; and
» in October, announcing a Nissan revival plan intended to achieve lasting and profitable growth for the company worldwide and, specifically, to return it to profitability in the financial year ending 2001.

Nissan's chief operating officer, Carlos Ghosn stressed that: "Although cost cutting will be the most dramatic and visible part of the plan, we cannot save our way to success."

The key points of the plan were, therefore, twofold.

» Increasing revenue by expanding its model range in the US and Japan and completely replacing its models in Europe.
» Reducing costs in three major areas:
  » global purchasing:
  » manufacturing; and
  » sales, general and administrative costs.

Here, we can focus on he company's plans to reduce costs through changes to the operations process, looking in turn at the three areas mentioned above.

Global purchasing

This represented some 60% of the company's total costs. The intention was to centralize purchasing rather than operate under the previous regional/country by country policy. It was expected that costs would be reduced by 20% over three years, with the number of parts and materials suppliers reducing from the previous 1145 to some 600. Because each supplier that was left would be supplying more to the company, they will benefit from economies of scale in their own operations and Nissan also expected to share in these cost savings.

Nissan had always worked closely with suppliers, but this new plan envisaged purchasing, engineers and suppliers working even more closely together to identify best practice from around the world and even challenging their own already high standards in technology, quality, costs and delivery.

Specific research and development resources were to be allocated to working with suppliers to find further cost reduction opportunities. The aim was to integrate suppliers into the design and development process in order to reduce the gap between a model's launch in Japan and its roll out in overseas markets.

Manufacturing efficiency

Although Nissan's manufacturing plants achieved very high productivity, the company recognized that it was providing too much capacity and that there were too many fixed costs. Three car assembly plants in Japan were to close by 2001 and two engine operations by 2002, reducing the capacity in Japan by 30%. At the same time, the rest of the manufacturing operation would be simplified. Previously, there had been 24 lines at seven assembly plants, while the new arrangements would reduce these to 15 over four plants by 2002 and further down to 12 across the four plants by 2004.

Sales, general and administrative costs

These were to be reduced by 20% by a range of measures, including cutting incentives, reducing bureaucracy, rationalizing advertising and reducing the dealer network by 10% in Japan, with further rationalization of the dealer network in the US to follow. Financial operations and controls would also change from regional to global. Both of the following measures were aimed at releasing money back into the core business of making cars:

» Nissan aimed to reduce its inventory by a significant amount to reduce the amount of money tied up in stock; and
» it considered each of its investments in other companies on a cost benefit basis, relinquishing holdings where the money could be more profitably invested.

There were also to be ever closer links with the new partner, Renault, and this was expected to provide a synergy in research and development and many other areas, rather than duplication of effort.

Staff would be reduced by some 21,000. This was expected to be achieved by the following means:

» natural attrition such as retirements and people leaving to join non-core businesses;
» part time employment to give more flexibility; and
» early retirement.

There would also be performance related payments for successful managers, stock options could be offered and a worldwide career structure would be introduced. These measures were to have the effect of increasing motivation of the workforce.

The plan clearly shows Nissan employing nearly all of the concepts of good operational practice in their revival plan. We can also see some excellent practice in their management of their plant in Sunderland in the UK. Sunderland had been a very highly efficient plant since it was opened and Nissan had to make a decision between Sunderland and the Renault factory at Flins in France for the production of its new Micra model.

Part of the reason that Nissan chose to locate a major plant in Sunderland was the fact that the European commission recognizes the area as a "regional assisted area," which can qualify for regional aid. The European Commission did in fact authorize some £40 million in aid towards the costs of Nissan transforming the plant at Sunderland to make it able to produce the new Micra model.

The Sunderland plant also had a remarkable new technological development, that has been referred to as the "the virtual production line." It already produced some 334,000 cars per year on two production lines. The new technology allows it to produce three different car models, the Micra, the Primera and the Almera on its current two lines, saving the company the costs of installing a third line.

In July 2001 the plan was working well because Nissan has announced the meeting of the first objective, which was to return to profit in the year ending in 2001. In fact Nissan, with Renault, produced the best financial result in the company's history. Together, the two companies sold some five million cars, maintaining their position in the top six car manufacturers.

Mr Ghosn suggests that the company is excited by what it has achieved and it knows that it can achieve still more: "We have moved from the emergency room to the recovery room."

TIMELINE

» **1912**: Datsun established.
» **1933**: Name changed to Nissan.
» **1960**: Awarded the Deming Prize for engineering excellence.
» **1960**: Nissan established itself in the international market.
» **1970s**: Fuel crises gives advantage to fuel-efficient Japanese cars.
» **1988**: Nissan brand used for all models.
» **1999**: Partnership with Renault.
» **1999**: Nissan revival plan.
» **2001**: Best profits ever recorded.

KEY INSIGHTS FROM THE CASE STUDY

Nissan has demonstrated the following operational concepts:

» The advantages of strategic partnerships.
» The importance of working closely with suppliers.

» The advantages of taking a global approach.
» The need to manage capacity.
» The need for continuous improvement and innovation.
» The introduction of the latest technology.
» The advantages of simplifying the operation.
» The need to reduce stock levels.
» The recognition of the lost financial opportunity costs of holding stock.
» The importance of motivating staff.
» The advantages of using part time working.
» The need to take into account a variety of factors when deciding where to locate plant and production lines, including governmental support.

In the following case study we will be looking at how easyJet has benefited from a policy decision to keep things simple and to standardize as far as possible to ensure costs are kept as low as possible.

CASE STUDY: EASYJET

The company was set up in 1995 by Stelios Haji-Ioannou with a mission to make air travel more affordable to more people. Its mission statement talks of "safe, good value, point to point air services" and defines its target markets as "leisure and business markets on a range of European routes."

From a standing start it has grown into an airline which carries over six million people per year, with passenger figures more than trebling since 1998, the first year it started selling seats over the Internet. It actually launched its Website in 1997, but did not commence taking online bookings until the following year.

When it first began to offer flights from Luton to Edinburgh and Glasgow it operated as more or less a virtual airline in that it leased two airplanes and contracted in all staff, including flight crew, cabin crew and check-in staff. It didn't own any aircraft of its own until 1996, when it began to fly internationally, commencing with Luton to Amsterdam.

The current fleet consists of some 21 Boeing 737s (18 type 300s and three of the newer type 700s) and by the end of 2004 is expected to number 44. None of the airplanes is currently more than five years old and even these relatively new aircraft will be phased out as new ones enter service so that the average age of the fleet stays very low. This reassures people that they are flying in the latest, up to date airplanes and it also reduces the company's operating costs as newer airplanes are more fuel-efficient and require less maintenance than older ones.

This focus on standardization is important as it is a key feature of the airline's ability to keep costs down, which, in turn, allows it to offer such low fares. This policy enables easyJet to reduce the complexity of its maintenance operation and avoids the necessity of keeping spares for a lot of different types of aircraft. It provides for economies of scale when bulk buying parts across the whole fleet. All aircraft are also painted in the same colors.

The policy also reduces training requirements for flight and cabin crews, who only have to learn how to operate one type of aircraft. Every member of the crew has to have knowledge of how to operate the airplane from their own job's perspective, especially in relation to the safety aspects. Using only one type of aircraft significantly reduces the amount of training needed.

In addition, this policy also avoids the need to roster crew regularly on a particular type of airplane in order to maintain their currency on it, thus reducing the complexity, and therefore, costs of crew rosters.

The airline does not issue any tickets to passengers, which also brings a large cost saving. There is also a free seating policy which reduces the complexity of the operation for the check-in staff and also avoids lengthy transactions at the check-in desk, which can lead to long queues being formed.

As a low cost airline, it offers a "no frills" service, which removes the need for complex catering activities that regular airlines have to manage. Seats are sold via the telephone (the telephone number is painted on the side of each airplane) and through the Internet, which are both very economical ways of delivering the service to customers. As mentioned above, after selling the first seat online in 1997, Internet bookings now account for some 85% of all seats sold. Seats purchased more than two months before the departure date can only be bought via the Internet.

All of the routes that easyJet flies are point to point, which means no transfers of baggage (and people) from one airplane to another. This is a relatively complex operation and an area where regular airlines are particularly vulnerable to breakdowns and failures. Some airlines even transfer baggage (and people) between different terminals as well as different airplanes; in addition, some of the alliances transfer them between member airlines too.

It is, perhaps, a very significant fact that Rod Eddington, the new chief executive of British Airways has decided that the services from London Gatwick, which have traditionally been a main hub for the airline with a lot of transfer traffic, will focus more on point to point services serving the people of the south-east of England.

It is also illuminating to look at the development of the company's route network. For operations they chose to base themselves at Luton Airport, a much cheaper option than one of the major airports such as Heathrow or Gatwick. Initial flights were to Edinburgh and Glasgow, then Aberdeen. International flights began in 1997 with Amsterdam, followed by Nice and Barcelona. As the route network has grown, easyJet has opened up additional base airports, all at "lower cost" airports, with Liverpool being used for the first time in 1997 and becoming a true base with aircraft and crews based there in 1999.

At the end of 1997, easyJet offered flights to Geneva, which was the beginning of a new phase in the company's growth. At the beginning of 1998, it bought a share in a Swiss charter operation, TEA Basel AG, based at Basle, which was renamed easyJet Switzerland in 1999 and moved to Geneva, from where it offered services to Amsterdam, Nice and Barcelona. Geneva became easyJet's third base and the first outside the UK. In early 2001 a fourth base was opened at Amsterdam's Schiphol Airport, with flights to Belfast, Edinburgh and Nice. Recently, the company has started to offer flights from London Gatwick.

It can be seen that the route network has grown steadily as experience has been gained, and it is also apparent that the operation, in airline terms, is relatively simple compared to the very complex operations run by some of the larger airlines.

Michael Porter's (1985)[1] generic model of competitive advantage suggests that a company can gain advantage by four main strategies:

» cost leadership – low priced products in a broad range of market segments;
» cost focus – low priced products in a relatively narrow range of segments;
» differentiation – providing a lot of variety and additional features in a wide range of segments; and
» differentiation focus – providing variety and additional features in a narrow range.

It can be seen that easyJet is following a policy of cost focus, aiming for low priced products in a relatively narrow range of market segments (as their network increases the policy might even be argued as cost leadership). This can be contrasted with some of the regular, larger airlines, which tend to aim at differentiation or differentiation focus.

easyJet does have some significant competition, including the low priced carriers Buzz (owned by KLM), Ryanair and Go (recently sold off by British Airways), all of which offer no frills services. It is also emerging that some of the regular airlines are ready to offer lower fares to try to capture some of the market too.

However, even if the regular airlines begin to compete more on price by lowering their fares, they will still be offering some differentiation, such as meals, seat allocations, for example, and it will be interesting to see how far they will go in competing on price with the no frills carriers such as easyJet.

All of easyJet's operational policies are in line with the objective of keeping costs to the minimum and, therefore, offering low priced fares. The company also seems to be giving customers what they are expecting (conformance quality) since passenger numbers are growing.

In November 2000 the company floated successfully as a public company. It forecasts further success with passenger numbers rising rapidly and new airplanes on order to meet the forecast increase in capacity. The company has also announced that it hopes, in the very near future, to offer some flights for free at off peak times to ensure that a flight during that time doesn't fly with empty seats. It feels that it can bring in revenue for the seat by providing customers with entertainment in their seats via the Internet (for example, offering a pay per view football match). So, as long as the seat is filled, it will be providing income for the company even if the seat itself is provided free of charge.

This is an interesting development, not only because it is very innovative, but also because it starts to provide some differentiation from the other low priced carriers and it will be interesting to see whether they will follow easyJet's lead.

TIMELINE

» **1995**: March – easyJet set up.
» **1995**: October – first booking taken.
» **1995**: November – first flights from Luton.
» **1996**: April – first international flights.
» **1997**: April – Website launched.
» **1997**: October – Liverpool used for the first time.
» **1998**: March – easyJet buys TEA Basel.
» **1998**: April – first seat sold online.
» **1999**: July – first services originating from outside the UK (Geneva).
» **1999**: October – seats sold online pass one million mark.
» **2000**: June – three million seats sold online.
» **2000**: September – four million seats sold online.
» **2000**: November – easyJet floated on the stock exchange.

KEY INSIGHTS FROM THE CASE STUDY

easyJet has applied the following operational concepts:

» Following a cost focus (perhaps moving towards cost leadership) strategy.
» Setting up its operational processes so as to reduce costs as far as possible.
» Increasing route variety but maintaining the standardization of the resources being used.

» Using modern equipment to reduce maintenance and fuel costs.
» Keeping all operations as simple as possible.
» Avoiding complex operations such as full catering and transfers.
» Using the latest technology.
» Applying the virtual company approach.
» Taking a strategic partner.
» Investing in additional resources as demand increases.

In the next case study we can examine how two giants of the manufacturing industry recognize both the need and the value of becoming more environmentally focused, and see the benefits this brings to their operations.

CASE STUDY: FORD AND NESTLE

Let's look first at the US based Ford Motor Company, which, as Table 7.1 shows, has brand names from across the world.

Table 7.1   Ford's brand names from across the world.

Ford	Mercury	Kwik-Fit
Volvo	Jaguar	Hertz
Mazda	Aston Martin	Quality Care
Lincoln	Land Rover	Ford Credit

It is important to look at:

» the company values in respect of the environment;
» how the company intends to display those values; and
» what the company has done so far and the benefits it has gained.

The messages about the company values come from the very top of the organization. Bill Ford the chairman stresses the need for "corporate citizenship," by which he means that the company should be a good neighbor to the environment. However, not only does he stress the fact that good citizenship brings value to the rest of society, he also feels strongly that it brings value to shareholders. The aim is to set up measures to show how this additional value can be identified.

At the 2000 Greenpeace Business Conference, Bill Ford said, in relation to global warming, that: "Transparency, stakeholder engagement and accountability with measures and standards will be the real regulatory tools of the twenty-first century and consumers will be the regulators."

Henry Wallace, the chief financial officer also said that: "Corporate citizenship generates value for shareholders and society. Our challenge is to define, measure and communicate that value."

One example that the men point to is the fact that improvements in fuel economy in autos not only reduces the use of gasoline, but generates extra sales as a result, thus benefiting shareholders. To show how it intends to meet these values, Ford has set out a health and environmental policy. Here are some of the key points:

» the company will at least meet the regulatory requirements in relation to health and environment, but will also seek to exceed them in some cases, by establishing their own even higher standards;
» environmental decisions will not be made on cost alone, but on greatest practical benefit;
» company products, services, processes and facilities are planned as far as practicable to minimize the creation of waste, pollution and other adverse impacts; and
» protection of health and environment is a company wide responsibility in which every employee must play their part.

Ford has set specific milestones up to the end of 2001, which include:

» developing a better internal understanding of how corporate citizenship creates value for both society and the company;
» identifying some measures of how societal value creates shareholder value;
» launching a pilot program in one or more of their businesses to include corporate citizenship in planning operations;

» establishing working relationships with other companies to address some of the challenges that corporate citizenship brings;
» seeking input from the financial community, including analysts and portfolio managers to test their attitudes to the objectives;
» encouraging the support of socially responsible investors who might buy Ford stock; and
» carrying out market research to establish how the company's performance in corporate citizenship influences buyer decisions.

We can now take a look at some of the actions that Ford has taken so far.

Adoption of ISO 14000

By 1998, all of Ford's plants were certified to ISO 14000, the part of the standard which covers environmental management systems. Adoption of the management systems has resulted in significant benefits to the company. For example, its Lima Plant in the US saved nearly 757,000 liters in water usage per day after changing its systems.

Recycling

Ford has a pro-active policy on recycling and reusing materials. More than 1.8 tonnes of recycled materials are used in its plants worldwide. For every new product the company creates objectives for the use of recycled materials. Some examples include the following:

» used tires are used in floor mats;
» carpets are used in air cleaner assemblies;
» bottle tops are used in air conditioning components;
» plastic soft drinks bottles are used in grille reinforcements;
» spent batteries are used in splash shields; and
» old batteries are recycled into new batteries.

The company has set up a recycling action team (RAT) in the US and in Europe (E-RAT) to work with suppliers of recycled materials. In addition, in Germany, there is an incentive scheme to encourage owners of older vehicles, which have higher emissions, to recycle them and replace them with new Ford vehicles with lower emissions.

Ford further helps the environment by planting a tree for every vehicle recycled. All recyclable parts are salvaged from the recycled vehicles.

Hazardous materials

Ford has a policy on the use of hazardous materials and has a standard setting out to Ford staff and suppliers which substances must be restricted in use or excluded altogether from use in products and facilities. Examples include:

» withdrawal of switches containing mercury from Ford vehicles; and
» elimination of chromium during the pre-painting process.

Refurbishing manufacturing facilities

A good example is the Windsor Engine Plant in Ontario, Canada, which was refurbished by Ford in 1993, in a manner that took into account a wide range of environmental issues. A buffer zone was established around the plant, part of which was landscaped with trees and flowers, and part was turned into a park with soccer and baseball facilities. The company took special care during demolition and reconstruction that there was no pollution of the nearby Detroit River, by providing a waste water treatment plant to intercept any chemicals or oil that might be accidentally released.

So, it can be clearly seen that Ford views environmentally sound policies as wholly complementary to the task of satisfying their share-holders, as they benefit from increased sales and reduced operating costs.

TIMELINE

» **1993**: Windsor Engine Plant rebuilt.
» **1997**: Most facilities for pre-painting are chromium free.
» **1998**: All Ford plants 14000 certified.
» **2000**: Keynote speech at Greenpeace business conference.
» **2001**: Corporate citizenship report.
» **2001**: Specific milestones to be met.

We can now look at Nestle, which is in an entirely different industry, the food processing industry. The company was founded in 1867 at Vevey in Switzerland and now has 479 factories worldwide. Nescafe coffee, in particular, is one of their strongest brands, but it also processes a range of food, water and confectionery items.

Nestle's aim is to be eco-efficient, defined in its environmental progress report in 2000 as "maximizing the production of goods while, at the same time, minimizing consumption of resources and reducing waste and emissions," which, as well as being environmentally sound, is also effective operating practice. The company is a founding member of the World Business Council for Sustainable Development in Geneva and has followed the Business Charter for Sustainable Development of the International Chamber of Commerce since its publication in 1991.

Policy on the environment

Nestle first published a policy on the environment in 1991 in order to define its worldwide strategy. The policy was updated in 1999. The company had taken a positive view towards the environment for a long time before this, but this statement was intended to set out the policy in a systematic way. Subsequent to this, the company set up the Nestle Environmental Management System, which is being implemented throughout the whole operation and has a remit of:

» ensuring compliance with the environmental policy, legislation and internal operational standards;
» looking for continuous improvement of Nestle's environmental performance;
» achieving compatibility with voluntary international standards such as ISO 14000; and
» building mutual trust with consumers, business partners and governmental authorities.

To measure progress towards its eco-efficiency objectives, the company set up a systematic and uniform approach to assessing the environmental performance of its factories worldwide, by carrying out surveys in 1994 and 1997. Results were checked against objectives, new objectives were identified and new action plans put into operation. The performance indicators selected included the following:

» water consumption;
» energy consumption;
» waste water generation;
» greenhouse gases;
» air acidification potential;
» ozone depleting substances; and
» by products/waste generation.

Apart from setting out performance indicators, the company focuses particularly on:

» the usage of water;
» an integrated approach through the supply chain; and
» manufacturing processes.

The usage of water

Water is a key priority for Nestle as Figure 7.1 indicates.

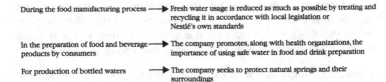

Fig. 7.1

An integrated approach through the supply chain

Nestle does not directly produce the raw materials for its processes. They are supplied either directly from producers or by trade channels. The company has set out some principles to protect the environment:

» all raw materials have to meet legal and internal quality requirements, including any limits on possible environmental contaminants;
» preference is usually given to materials produced by environmentally sound farming methods; and
» farmers are encouraged to apply sustainable farming methods.

Manufacturing processes

The manufacturing processes of the company all aim to:

» use raw materials, water and energy efficiently;
» minimize the use of environmentally detrimental substances;
» seek improvements in efficiency; and
» reduce waste generation and emissions.

We can look at some examples of Nestle putting their policy into practice. Solid waste, instead of being put in landfill sites, is now being recycled.

» Coffee grounds, produced during the manufacture of instant coffee are being used as fuel. In a factory in Malaysia, for example, approximately every 100 tonnes of coffee grounds replaces 40 tonnes of fuel.
» Sludges and by-products are being used for fertilizer. In a factory in Connecticut, US, the latest technology compost facility turns liquid and solid wastes into a soil additive.

Nestle operates 10 co-generation power plants across the world which are significantly more efficient than conventional power plants, resulting in both a reduction in energy consumption and a reduction of emissions into the atmosphere. An example is the Gerona plant in Spain where the system reduced gas consumption by approximately 3600 tonnes of oil equivalent and decreased emissions by 800 tonnes per year.

Nestle is also committed to phase out the use of chlorofluorocarbons and has reduced its chlorofluorocarbon emissions by 80% since 1986. The company provides information on its environmental activities and has set up an Internet site. It also communicates with:

» governments;
» local communities;
» industry;
» consumers;
» other stakeholders; and
» its own staff.

Nestle 2000 progress review showed all performance indicators moving significantly in the right direction.

TIMELINE

» **1991**: Environmental policy set out.
» **1991**: Nestle environmental management system set up.
» **1994**: Factory surveys sent out.
» **1995**: Special report shows progress in the previous five years.
» **1996**: Website set up to share information.
» **1997**: Further factory surveys sent out.
» **1999**: Environmental policy updated.
» **1999**: Website expanded.
» **2000**: Environment progress report produced.

KEY INSIGHTS FROM THE CASE STUDY

Both Ford and Nestle have applied the following operational concepts:

» Working closely with suppliers.
» Working together with stakeholders.
» Reducing energy used in the manufacturing process.
» Permeating policy throughout the whole company.
» Taking a global view.
» Being concerned about the environment and its sustainability.
» Using waste products as useful inputs to other operations processes.
» Setting out clear performance objectives.

NOTES

1 Porter, M.E. (1985) *Competitive Advantage: Creating and Sustaining Superior Performance*, The Free Press, New York.

Key Concepts and Thinkers

Operations and technology has a very wide range of concepts. This chapter includes a glossary of the terms that are used. It includes:

» explanations of the most common terms, grouped around several key concepts; and

» key writers and thinkers.

This chapter will explain briefly some of the terms used in the study of operations management and technology. They have been set out and grouped around a few key areas:

» capacity;
» health and safety;
» materials management;
» operations process;
» planning tools; and
» quality.

CAPACITY

Bottlenecks – a part of the operation that has less capacity than other parts of the operation, causing a backlog in the process.

Capacity – the amount of product that the operation can produce in a given time.

Differential pricing – charging different prices at different times to manipulate the demand for a product.

Smoothing – creating more of a product during a period of low demand and storing it for use when demand is higher.

HEALTH AND SAFETY

Health and safety at work legislation – most countries have their own legislation covering the employer's and the employee's responsibilities at the work place. These will cover areas such as:

» contractors' and visitors' safety;
» manual handling (such as lifting heavy items);
» provision of personal protective equipment (such as protective glasses);
» working environment (such as requirements for space and toilets);
» operating equipment and machinery (such as providing guard rails and carrying out maintenance);
» display screens (such as computer monitors);
» substances hazardous to health;
» organizational policies (on smoking for example);

» first aid requirements;
» fire precautions; and
» staff safety representation.

MATERIALS MANAGEMENT

Annual requirement value – the amount that will be spent on using a particular item in a year (number used multiplied by its cost).

Bill of materials – a product exploded into its component parts.

Buffer (or safety) *stock* – the amount of a particular item of stock that must be maintained to ensure the supply does not run out.

Dependent items – those items of which requirements can be directly related to the number of products that will be produced.

Economic *order* **quantity** – a formula based on the fact that the total cost of an order is made up of the cost of placing the order plus the cost of carrying the stock when it arrives. The larger the quantity that is ordered at one time, the less the order-placing costs will be (because there will be fewer orders in a given time), but the carrying costs will be higher (because there will be more stock to look after). The smaller the quantity that is ordered at one time, the greater will be the order placing costs (because there will be more orders in a given time, but the carrying costs will be less (through carrying less stock). At some level of order quantity for any organization, the carrying and the ordering costs will be equal and this is the economic order quantity. Although this can be a useful formula, especially in complex organizations, it does not take account of the following factors:

» a significantly fluctuating demand; and
» supplier discounts for larger quantities.

Independent items – those items of which requirements are not directly linked to the number of products that will be produced; these are analyzed in more detail in Chapter 6.

Inventory – all of the materials used by an organization, including raw materials, work in progress and finished products.

Just-in-time – a system intended to operate without maintaining stock.

Lead time – the length of time between ordering an item and its being available for use by the organization.

MRP I - a forward planning system for managing materials throughout the operations process, usually computer controlled.

MRP II - a more sophisticated form of MRP I, which also links in invoicing, bills payment and financial information.

Pareto/ABC analysis - The Pareto rule (known as the 80/20 rule) suggests that 80% of the total cost of materials will relate to just 20% of the items. Using the annual requirements value of each item, as mentioned above, the organization can identify the top 20%. These will be considered the "A" items, which will need to be rigorously controlled.

It is likely that the next 30% or so of the items will account for another 15% of the yearly total; these will be "B" items, which will be controlled, but not to the same extent as "A" items. The final 50% of items will probably only account for about 5% of the yearly total and they will be "C" items; it will not be cost-effective for the organization to invest too much money or resources in controlling these.

Re-order level - the level of stock at which the next order should be placed.

True cost of ownership - the total amount that it will cost to keep an item in stock, including all of the costs associated with it, such as storage, security and disposal.

THE OPERATIONS PROCESS

CAD/CAM - computer aided design/computer aided manufacture.

Customer - anyone for whom a goods or service product is provided.

Inputs - anything that goes into the operations process, including raw materials, information and people.

Operating systems - the types of system that are used to turn inputs into finished products; the five main types are analyzed in Chapter 6.

Outputs - anything that results from the operations process, including finished products, rejects and waste.

Robotics - using a machine, which, once set up, will perform tasks, or a series of tasks, without further human intervention.

Supplier - anyone who provides a service or delivers a goods product.

Transformation process - the process used to change inputs into outputs, as discussed in Chapter 2.

PLANNING TOOLS

Aggregate planning – working out the long-term size of the operation in terms of capacity, people, plant, machines and location.

Contingency plans – a plan that is held in reserve in case the original plan is not effective.

Gantt chart – a chart, such as in Figure 8.1, that plots activities against time, showing when each specific activity should begin and end.

	Jan	Feb	March	April	May
Task 1	████	████	██		
Task 2		██	████	█	
Task 3				█	████

Fig. 8.1

In the Gantt chart the first task begins in January and is scheduled to be completed midway through March. The second task begins while task one is still in progress and continues until mid-April. The third task begins in mid-April and is to be completed by the end of May. The chart does not show, however, whether the second task has to be completed before the third task can begin, which is one of the limitations of the Gantt chart.

Loading – the process of allocating time and resources to a particular task.

Network analysis – a diagram that plots events and activities, and identifies any relationships or linkages between them. There are several forms:

» Critical path analysis – shows how long each activity will take and its relationship with other events and activities, identifying which activities cannot start before another has been completed (for example, the electric wiring can't be installed until the house walls have been erected).

» PERT analysis – adds the additional refinement of recognizing that activities have a "shortest possible time, longest time and most likely time" and takes account of these in the process.

» Critical path method – also identifies the effects of different resources on the length of time activities take (and on the cost!), allowing the project manager to prioritize resources if activities overrun.

Scheduling – setting specific dates against tasks.

Sequencing – working out the order in which tasks need to be performed.

QUALITY

Conformance quality – relates to whether a product meets its design specifications and does what it is supposed to do.

Continuous improvement – pro-actively seeking ways of improving processes, systems, people and products.

Design quality – additional specifications designed into the product to satisfy the needs of a specific market segment.

Fail-safe – ensuring that, if any item fails, it results in a safe situation; for example, if a railway signal light is out, a driver will regard it as a stop signal.

International quality standard – internationally recognized marks of quality such as ISO 9000 (management systems) and the new environmental standard ISO 14000.

Preventative maintenance – carrying out regular maintenance to ensure that machines and equipment do not break down.

Process control – setting up systems to ensure that the quality of a product is monitored during its production process and any remedial action is taken.

Quality assurance – setting up systems throughout the whole organization to ensure that everyone knows what their own responsibilities are in respect of the quality of the organization's products.

Quality circles – small work groups made up of people from a variety of functions in an organization; their objective is to analyze problems and find solutions, or simply find better ways of doing things.

Sampling – taking a sample of a product to check whether it meets quality standards.

Standardization – reducing the variety of items or systems used in the operations process to reduce costs.

Standards – the quality specifications that a product must meet; examples can be found in Chapter 6.

Statistical process control – measurements are taken throughout the production process and compared with the targeted quality levels; any trends are analyzed and, if the results show that there is likely to be a failure to meet the intended quality levels, remedial action will be taken.

KEY THINKERS

Frederick W. Taylor

Frederick Winslow Taylor was the pioneer of scientific management, which focused on finding the most effective way of carrying jobs out. This was the origin of time and method study. He was born in Philadelphia and passed the Harvard entrance examinations, but poor eyesight prevented him from pursuing his studies and he became an apprentice at Enterprise Hydraulics, a pump works in Philadelphia. After he completed his apprenticeship, he went to Midvale Steel Company, where he worked his way up to chief engineer by 1884. He then became a consultant, working with a number of important companies.

In 1898, he was consultant to the Bethlehem Steel Company in Pennsylvania, where he investigated methods of shoveling materials into the furnaces. A variety of materials had to be input by teams of workers and each person used their own shovel. Taylor found that different materials could be loaded more effectively with a specially designed shovel for that material. Using the right shovel for the type of material allowed the workers to increase the amount of work they did, thus increasing their earnings as they were paid directly in proportion to what they did.

He was a rather controversial figure at the time and many people resented his methods, which assumed that people were only motivated to work hard in return for money. His methods also left the individual with very little leeway to use their own initiative. Nevertheless, his work had a very great influence on the management of operations and several leading thinkers of the day built upon his pioneering work.

Highlights

Books:

» (1911) *The Principles of Scientific Management,* Harper, New York.

Elton Mayo

Elton Mayo introduced the human face of operations, considering how people reacted to their working conditions and how important job satisfaction was. He carried out a series of experiments over a period of eight years from 1924-32 at the former Hawthorne Works of the Western Electric Company (which eventually became AT&T). He was able to demonstrate that the way people worked was affected by a whole range of complex factors including:

» how they were supervised;
» team interaction;
» how important they were made to feel by the organization; and
» interaction and co-operation with each other.

Highlights

Experiments:

» *1924-27 illumination experiments* - in which it was expected that increases in the illumination in a department would increase productivity. In fact, they found that productivity increased during the experiment irrespective of whether the light was brightened or dimmed.
» *1927-32 relay-assembly test room experiments* - in which a small group of women were given a separate test room to work in; changes were made to their breaks and workday lengths. Each time a change was made they had an input into the decision. They also started to make their own self-supervising decisions about the work. It was found that output from the group increased markedly.
» *1931-32 bank wiring observation room experiments* - in which a group of men were set to work in a test room. The group had their own ideas about how much output there should be each day and everyone was expected to conform, doing neither too much nor too little.

Dr W. Edwards Deming

Dr W. Edwards Deming was one of the several very distinguished figures who played a major part in the focus on quality. He gained his doctorate in physics from Yale University, though his main interests were statistics and quality control. He started his own practice in 1946.

Although the Japanese are often credited with the first application of quality methods, they were, themselves, inspired by Dr Deming, who visited the country several times to give his advice. He was given numerous honors for his work, both by the president of the United Sates and by the emperor of Japan.

The Deming Prize was set up by the Japanese in 1951 in his honor, and is awarded to companies that can demonstrate the application of company wide quality schemes. He wrote several books, the two most important being *Out of the Crisis*, in which he set out his 14–point plan for quality, and The *New Economics*. He also wrote 171 papers. Deming's 14–point plan suggested the following:

» Everyone in the organization should focus on improving the product.
» As times change, organizations must change their philosophy.
» Quality should be built into a product rather than rely upon inspections to find any faults.
» Long-term relationships with suppliers should be built, based upon loyalty and trust.
» The organization should aim for continuous improvement in production systems.
» People should be properly trained.
» The aim of leadership should be to help people to do their jobs better.
» Fear should be banished so that people can work effectively.
» A team-working environment should be created among the various departments.
» Exhorting people to work better through slogans simply leads to de-motivation because the problems usually lie in the system rather than in the workforce.
» Leadership should replace work quotas.
» People at all levels should be free to feel the joy of workmanship by focusing on quality rather than amounts of production.

» People should be provided with opportunities to develop their skills.
» Everyone should be involved in the change process.

Highlights

Books:

» (1986) *Out of the Crisis*, MIT Center for Advanced Engineering Study, Cambridge, Mass.
» (1994) *The New Economics: For Industry, Government, Education* MIT Center for Advanced Engineering Study, Cambridge, Mass.

Philip Crosby

Philip Crosby pioneered "zero defects" and "get things right first time." These would allow an organization to have high quality and low cost.

Highlights

Books:

» (1979) *Quality is Free: The Art of Making Quality Certain*, McGraw-Hill, New York.
» (1995) *Quality is Still Free: Making Quality Certain in Uncertain Times*, McGraw-Hill, New York.

Joseph Juran

Joseph Juran lectured extensively in Japan, like W. Edwards Deming. He published a definitive work on quality control in 1951, which is now in its fifth edition. He pioneered the view that the true test of quality is fitness for use.

Highlights

Institutes:
The Juran Institute was set up in 1979 and its headquarters are in Washington, DC.

Books:

» (1999) *The Quality Control Handbook* 5th edn, Duran, J.M. & Blanton Godfrey, A., McGraw-Hill, New York.

» (1989) *Juran on Leadership for Quality: An Executive Handbook*, The Free Press, New York.

» (1992) *Juran on Quality by Design: The New Steps for Planning Quality into Goods and Services*, The Free Press, New York.

Papers and lectures:

» There are numerous papers and lectures including those delivered in Japan, which are available from the Juran Institute.

Kaoru Ishikawa

Kaoru Ishikawa was president of Musashi Institute of Technology in Tokyo and a professor at Tokyo University. He pioneered the use of quality circles and statistical process control. He also created the "cause and effect diagram" (also known as the fishbone diagram), which was a very useful technique in problem solving, a simplified example of which is shown in Figure 8.2.

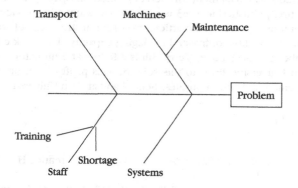

Fig. 8.2 Kaoru Ishikawa's cause and effect diagram.

The main bones of a fish are drawn with the problem set out at the head. Each bone represents an area that may be contributing to the problem. Smaller bones on these larger bones represent factors within a particular area. The problem is systematically analyzed area by area and all of the relevant factors that are contributing to the problem are identified. Remedial action can then be taken.

Highlights

Books:

» (1972) *Guide to Quality Control*, Asian Productivity Organization, Tokyo.
» (1985) *What is Total Quality Control? The Japanese Way*, Prentice Hall, New York.

Techniques:

» Cause and effect diagram.

Terry Hill

Terry Hill has made a major contribution to the study and application of operations management. His book *Production/Operations Management*, first published in 1983 is a classic work covering a wide range of operational topics. It is particularly strong in the areas of strategy, time study, quality control and managing capacity. The book contains a number of case studies. Terry Hill is a fellow at Templeton College, Oxford University. Prior to this role, he was professor of operations management at London Business School and at Bath University.

Highlights

Books:

» (1983) *Production/Operations Management*, Prentice Hall, Hemel Hempstead.
» Hill, T. (1993) *Essence of Production/Operations Management*, Prentice Hall, Hemel Hempstead.
» Hill, T. (1999) *Manufacturing Strategy Text and Cases*, McGraw-Hill Higher Education, Hemel Hempstead.

Resources

Sets out the best resources for operations and technology, including:

» books and articles; and
» Websites.

BOOKS AND ARTICLES

Basalla, G. (1989) *Evolution of Technology*, CUP, Cambridge.

Bedeian, A.G. (1989) *Management*, The Dryden Press, New York.

Bignell, V. (1985) *Manufacturing Systems: Context, Applications and Techniques*, Blackwell, Oxford.

Cartwright, R. & Green, G. (1996) *In Charge of Customer Satisfaction* Blackwell, Oxford.

Clutterbuck, D. (1992) *Actions Speak Louder: Management Guide to Corporate Social Responsibility*, Kogan Page, London.

Crosby, P.B. (1979) *Quality is Free: The Art of Making Quality Certain*, McGraw-Hill, New York.

Crosby, P.B. (1995) *Quality is Still Free: Making Quality Certain in Uncertain Times*, McGraw-Hill, New York.

Dear, A. (1988) *Working Towards Just-in-Time*, Kogan Page, London.

Deming, W.E. (1986) *Out of the Crisis*, MIT Center for Advanced Engineering Study, Cambridge, Mass.

Deming, W.E. (1994) *The New Economics: For Industry, Government, Education*, MIT Center for Advanced Engineering Study, Cambridge, Mass.

Drucker, P.F. *et al.* (1991) *Managing the Non-Profit Organization: Principles and Practices*, Harper Business, New York.

Fayol, H. (1916) *General and Industrial Administration*, Pitman, London.

Handy, C. (1976) *Understanding Organizations*, Penguin, London.

Handy, C. (1989) *The Age of Unreason*, Business Books, London.

Hannigan, T. (1995) *Management Concepts and Practices* (Chapters 12 and 14), Pitman, London.

Harrison, M. (1993) *Operations Management Strategy*, Pitman, Harlow.

Herzberg, F. (1966) *Work and the Nature of Man*, Staples Press, New York.

Hill, T. (1983) *Production/Operations Management*, Prentice Hall, Hemel Hempstead.

Hill, T. (1993) *Essence of Production/Operations Management*, Prentice Hall, Hemel Hempstead.

Hill, T. (1999) *Manufacturing Strategy Text and Cases*, McGraw-Hill Higher Education, Hemel Hempstead.

Ishikawa, K. (1972) *Guide to Quality Control*, Asian Productivity Organization, Tokyo.

Ishikawa, K. (1985) *What is Total Quality Control? The Japanese Way*, Prentice Hall, New York.

Juran, J.M. (1989) *Juran on Leadership for Quality: An Executive Handbook*, The Free Press, New York.

Juran, J.M. (1992) *Juran on Quality by Design: The New Steps for Planning Quality into Goods and Services*, The Free Press, New York.

Juran, J.M. (1999) *The Quality Control Handbook* 5th edn, Duran, J.M. & Blanton Godfrey, A., McGraw-Hill, New York.

Koontz, H. & Weihrich, H. (1988) *Management* (Part 6), McGraw-Hill, New York.

Maslow, A. (1943) "A theory of human motivation." *Psychological Review*, vol 50, No. 4.

McGregor, D. (1960) *The Human Side of Enterprise*, McGraw-Hill, New York.

Needle, D. (1989) *Business in Context* (Chapter 6), Chapman and Hall, London.

Ohmae, K. (1982) *The Mind of The Strategists*, McGraw-Hill, New York.

Peters, T. & Waterman, R.H. (1982) *In Search of Excellence: Lessons from America's Best-Run Companies*, Harper & Row, New York.

Peters, T. (1987) *Thriving on Chaos*, Pan Books, London.

Peters, T. (1994) *Pursuit of Wow! Every Person's Guide to Topsy-Turvey Times*, Macmillan, London.

Porter, M.E. (1985) *Competitive Advantage: Creating and Sustaining Superior Performance*, The Free Press, New York.

Schroeder, R.G. (1989) *Operations Management: Decision Making in the Operations Function*, McGraw-Hill International, New York.

Slack, N. Chambers, S. & Johnston, R. (2001) *Operations Management*, Pitman, Harlow.

Slater, R. (1990) *Quantitative Techniques in a Business Context*, Chapman & Hall, London.

Taylor, F.W. (1911) *The Principles of Scientific Management*, Harper, New York.

Thompson, J.L. (1990) *Strategic Management* (Chapter 11), Alden Press, Oxford.

Trompenaars, F. (1993) *Riding the Waves of Culture*, Economist Books, London.

Turner, J.R. (1993) *Handbook of Project-Based Management: Improving the Processes for Achieving Strategic Objectives*, McGraw-Hill, New York.

Weber, M. (1947) *The Theory of Social and Economic Organization*, tr. Henderson, A.M. & Parsons, T., Oxford University Press, Oxford.

Wild, R. (1985) *Essentials of Production and Operations Management*, Holt, Rinehart & Winston, London.

WEBSITES

A number of Websites have been used in researching this book and the case studies. Here are some you might find interesting:

- » www.airbus.com
- » www.britishairways.com
- » www.coca-cola.com
- » www.delta.com
- » www.easyjet.com
- » www.egg.com
- » www.ford.com
- » www.landsend.com
- » www.mcdonalds.com
- » www.nestle.com
- » www.nissan-global.com
- » www.starbucks.com

The Harvard, Baker Library site is very interesting, too, as a lot of information about trade bodies and associations can be accessed without subscribing, though more facilities are available by subscription.

MAGAZINES

Professional Engineering is a very interesting magazine published twice monthly, except August and December. It discusses the latest technological advances in industry and is especially strong on design. It is available, on subscription, from the Institution of Mechanical Engineers, 1 Birdcage Walk, London, SW1H 9JJ.

INSTITUTES

The following institutes have Websites from which a number of linked sites can be accessed:

» Manufacturing Management and Technology Institute: www.manu-facturing.net
» The Customer Care Institute: www.customercare.com
» The Institute of Management: www.inst-mgt.org.uk

Ten Steps to Making Operations Work

Provides 10 key steps to make the concepts work which are:

- » be clear about what the product is;
- » identify any special characteristics;
- » forecast demand and the pattern of demand;
- » plan to meet the demand;
- » identify the technology;
- » select suppliers and partners;
- » decide your attitude towards inventory/stock holding;
- » take a positive approach to quality;
- » motivate your staff; and
- » be environmentally friendly.

In the preceding chapters we have looked at some of the key concepts that should help organizations to deliver their products. As we mentioned in Chapter 1, they apply to any organization, not just commercial companies which are seeking to make a profit. They apply just as much to charitable organizations, governments and other not-for-profit organizations. If there is any doubt about this, you just need to listen to politicians talking about "the party machine" or recognize the police "operations room" in any film. The very word "operation" is used to describe the activities of a surgeon.

Whatever type of organization you belong to and whichever department you work in, these key concepts should provide you with some guidance as to the key areas upon which you need to focus.

Let's now consider 10 steps that anyone can take to ensure that they deliver consistently high quality products. All of the steps are inter-related in that decisions you make in one step will affect the decisions made in another.

1. BE CLEAR ABOUT WHAT THE PRODUCT IS

It is important that the people who are producing the final product have a very clear idea of what the specification is in terms of design quality. This will be driven by customer preferences and is one of the decisions that the person who is responsible for marketing will take.

If people are not clear about what the product is, they may disappoint the customer by providing something different. Staff should be given clear guidelines about which types of operational decisions are within their remit and which should be referred to their manager. They should also be given training in how to exercise this responsibility. This will enable them to "go the extra mile" for customers without impacting adversely on the costs of the organization.

Smiles and courtesy and a willingness to help customers should be part of the standard product.

The appropriate resources and technology should be available to staff to enable them to deliver the product consistently to a high standard.

2. IDENTIFY ANY SPECIAL CHARACTERISTICS

We saw in Chapter 6 that some service and goods products have special characteristics and may need special management in some way; this may be even more the case if the products are being manufactured, delivered or distributed on a global basis, as we saw in Chapter 5.

It is important that these characteristics are recognized. For example, it was noticeable that services may be delivered in a slightly different manner by different people at different times; it is clear that significant effort will need to be invested in training staff to deliver services, including sessions where they share their different experiences. Again, if products can't be stored because they are perishable, for example, strategies need to be in place for ensuring that they are all sold before they become worthless.

3. FORECAST DEMAND AND THE PATTERN OF DEMAND

Some estimate of the overall demand for the product needs to be established. However, the overall demand, in itself, will not be enough, because there may be seasonal, geographic or some other type of fluctuation that might be important.

Processing 3000 tonnes of fresh fruit in a year is a quite different proposition from processing it in the space of two months, and would need a significantly different arrangement of resources. The same point would apply, if the processing took place in several different countries.

There are many other products that can be classed as seasonal apart from fruit, including those sold in connection with religious festivals or specific sporting events. For example, one of the key issues for those countries which host the Olympic Games is that they have to build stadiums and facilities for one specific set of events which they may never hold again. Many countries have problems afterwards because the running costs are high in relation to the lower level of activities that are subsequently available.

4. PLAN TO MEET THE DEMAND

Once realistic estimates of the pattern of demand are available, the task of planning to meet the demand can follow. As we saw, in Chapter 6, these plans will be a mix of long, medium- and short-term. The crucial decisions that need to be made are:

» what size the organization will be in terms of the fixed assets such as buildings, staff, machines and storage space;
» where it will be located;
» whether the customer will be involved in the delivery; and
» what technology will be used.

These aspects are particularly important if the organization is operating globally.

Depending on the type of product, the size could be anything from a network of inter-related factories on a global scale, to a network of high street outlets across the world, to a person using a computer in their spare room.

We saw, in Chapter 3, that Handy suggests that many organizations will have a much smaller size in future and employ strategies to increase the resources as demand requires. This may mean hiring workers or machines when necessary. This offers greater flexibility than traditional approaches. It also puts more focus on the medium- and short-term strategies for managing capacity that we saw in Chapter 6.

5. IDENTIFY THE TECHNOLOGY

It will be necessary to decide which type of operating system you will be using to suit your type of product, in addition to identifying the people, the technology and the systems that will be needed.

There are three absolute constants about technology:

» it will continually be updated, so it can very quickly become less effective and may become obsolete;
» people need to be trained to use it and any updates that follow; and
» what you have today, your competitors will probably have an even better version of tomorrow.

However, it does not follow that you need to update your technology every five minutes. Some of it is much too complex and expensive and may take a long time to design in any case. Rather, its renewal or replacement needs to be built into your operational plan in a controlled way. Using this approach the financial resources can be planned ahead and the training of staff can be completed in time for implementation.

In some cases, the old technology you are using may suit your own particular organization's operation better than the new; or it may link into your customer's systems more effectively. However, it will certainly be worthwhile keeping an eye on what technology your competitors are using.

6. SELECT SUPPLIERS AND PARTNERS

Before suppliers can be selected, a decision must be made about how much the organization will make or provide for itself and how much will need to be provided by external suppliers. This is the traditional "make or buy" decision.

While others may argue that using several suppliers ensures they compete with each other to provide the organization with the best quality at the keenest prices, a TQM approach suggests working together with a smaller number of trusted suppliers, as Nissan are doing (Chapter 7).

The supply of scarce resources, such as high quality gems, precious metals, or high quality coffee beans, for example, will need special arrangements and agreements with particular suppliers. In some cases, the organization will buy up the supplies to ensure a continuous supply (common in the coffee and tea industries).

In some cases, rather than producing something yourself or having it provided by a supplier, it may be advantageous to consider a strategic alliance so that you are working together with another organization with each partner providing a part of the operation and each reaping the rewards of a job well done.

7. DECIDE YOUR ATTITUDE TO INVENTORY/STOCK HOLDING

A policy is needed on how much stock will be carried and how much of the finished product will be stored before it goes to the customer.

As discussed in Chapter 6 options range from the virtual organization, which keeps no stock itself and no finished products, to a just-in-time system (pull) to a full materials requirements planning system (push). Clearly the approach that is taken will have a major effect on decisions that are made in step four above in which the aggregate size of the business is set.

8. TAKE A POSITIVE APPROACH TO QUALITY

A decision will be needed on the approach that the organization will take towards ensuring the quality of its products. Will it rely on the customer to tell it when things have gone wrong or will it build quality into the process of producing its products?

Philip Crosby's work mentioned in Chapters 3 and 6 showed that a TQM approach could produce high quality products while keeping costs low, because of the savings made from avoiding the extra work associated with low quality.

It was also stressed in Deming's 14-point plan that quality measures should not just apply to the quotas that are produced, there should also be measures relating to customer satisfaction and several other aspects such as:

» size;
» strength;
» time within which;
» time without failure;
» appearance;
» taste; and
» on time.

Systems will need to be set up to ensure the quality of suppliers (and partners) and staff will need to be properly and regularly trained.

9. MOTIVATE YOUR STAFF

The work of Mayo, Maslow, Herzberg and others who investigated the factors that are likely to provide motivation for people at work, suggests that there is a lot that the organization can do to get the best out of its staff. Peters and Waterman suggest "productivity through people." Certainly, an approach allowing people to develop their skills and take on additional responsibility will enable them to give their best. Interesting work will also motivate them, while Taylor's scientific approach may lead to de-motivation and unrest.

Several theorists, notably Herzberg, have linked de-motivation to poor working conditions. This is why the most successful organizations pay particular attention to the design of any new buildings. The British Airways Headquarters Building at Waterside near Heathrow Airport is designed as a European style street with a central paved area with waterfalls and pavement cafes to the side. The working offices are built on each side of the street. There is always a buzz of energy as people carry out breakfast meetings over morning coffee.

The health and safety aspects are also important whether staff are working in a factory with a lot of potentially dangerous machinery, or working in an air-conditioned office. People can become complacent in an apparently safe environment and it is easy to trip over worn carpets or slip on wet floors. It is important that safety policies are known by the staff and are carried out.

Any organization seeking to use people working from home will have to take socialization needs into account and may have to provide regular meetings if they want to avoid the workers feeling isolated.

10. BE ENVIRONMENTALLY FRIENDLY

Any adverse environmental impact will need to be eliminated if the organization is to live in harmony with its neighbors. It is evident from the case study in Chapter 7 and from the efforts that the most successful companies are making in this area, that this is a real issue for the twenty-first century.

This may mean:

» avoiding waste spilling into the environment;
» reducing noise;
» recycling paper;
» reducing the use of coal and oil;
» reducing emissions from engines;
» using suppliers who take an environmentally responsible approach;
» funding research into environmental issues; and
» supporting research.

KEY LEARNING POINTS
The 10 steps for pulling it all together are:

» Be clear about what the product is.
» Identify any special characteristics.
» Forecast demand and the pattern of demand.
» Plan to meet the demand.
» Identify the technology.
» Select suppliers and partners.
» Decide your attitude towards inventory/stock holding.
» Take a positive approach to quality.
» Motivate your staff.
» Be environmentally friendly.

Frequently Asked Questions (FAQs)

Q1: I'm not in the operations department; does this mean I'm not involved in operations?

A: Whichever department they are working in, everyone is involved in operations as can be seen in Chapter 2.

Q2: We all know that manufactured goods are products, but are services products too?

A: Products can be either service or goods products. You can find out more in Chapter 6.

Q3: What is meant by Total Quality Management?

A: This is a system put in place to ensure that an organization produces high quality products consistently. It is discussed in Chapter 6.

Q4: What is a just-in time system?

A: It aims to reduce stock levels as far as possible and is discussed in more detail in Chapter 6.

Q5: Does the operations process adversely affect the environment?

A: Sometimes it can, and the best companies recognize their responsibilities in this area and are making great strides to be environmentally friendly. You can learn more in Chapter 6 and the case study in Chapter 7.

Q6: How can I manage fluctuations in demand for my products?

A: You can either manipulate the demand for or the supply of the product. Some strategies can be found in Chapter 6.

Q7: How can I use the Internet to make my operations more effective?

A: There are a number of strategies that are discussed in Chapter 4, where there is also a case study.

Q8: What is a quality circle?

A: This is a group of people from different departments who analyze issues and problems. They are usually found in TQM systems as can be seen in Chapter 6.

Q9: I want to offer my products abroad, should I consider a strategic partner?

A: This is certainly one strategy that could be considered; there are examples of organizations that have done this in Chapter 5.

Q10: What is ISO 14000?

A: It is an international standard, which relates to an organization's attitude towards the environment. It is explained in Chapter 6, though there are also references to it in Chapter 5 and in a case study in Chapter 7.

Index